Master Game Theory

Anticipate. Analyze. Decide with Authority.

Redefine Your Power in the Game of Life.

By Albert Rutherford

www.albertrutherford.com

albertrutherford@gmail.com

Copyright © 2024 by Albert Rutherford.

All rights reserved.

No part of this publication may be reproduced, stored in a retrieval system, or transmitted in any form or by any means, electronic, mechanical, photocopying, recording, scanning or otherwise, except as permitted under Section 107 or 108 of the 1976 United States Copyright Act, without the prior written permission of the author.

Limit of Liability/ Disclaimer of Warranty: The author makes no representations or warranties regarding the accuracy or completeness of the contents of this work and specifically disclaims all warranties, including without limitation warranties of fitness for a particular purpose. No warranty may be created or extended by sales or promotional materials. The advice and recipes contained herein may not be suitable for everyone. This work is sold with the understanding that the author is not engaged in rendering medical, legal or other professional advice or services. If professional assistance is required, the services of a competent professional person should be sought. The author shall not be liable for damages arising herefrom. The fact that an individual, organization of website is referred to in this work as a citation and/or potential source of further information does not mean that the author endorses the information the individual, organization to the website may provide or recommendations they/it may make. Further, readers should be aware that Internet websites listed in this work might have changed or disappeared between when this work was written and when it is read.

For general information on the products and services or to obtain technical support, please contact the author.

I have a gift for you…

Thank you for choosing my book, Practice Game Theory! I would like to show my appreciation for the trust you gave me by giving The Art of Asking Powerful Questions – in the World of Systems to you!

In this booklet you will learn:

-what bounded rationality is,

-how to distinguish event- and behavior-level analysis,

-how to find optimal leverage points,

-and how to ask powerful questions using a systems thinking perspective.

Visit www.albertrutherford.com to claim your gift: The Art of Asking Powerful Questions in the World of Systems

Table of Contents

I have a gift for you… 7

Chapter 1: How Game Theory Saved My Life 13

History 16

Chapter 2: Thinking Like a Smart Prisoner in Times of Crisis 27

History 30
How It Works 31
Surviving The Next Pandemic with Prisoner's Dilemma 37
Solving The Prisoner's Dilemma In Everyday Life 40

Chapter 3: A Beautiful Blunder 43

History 45
How it Works 49
Limitations 52
Case Study and Significance of Nash Equilibrium 55

Chapter 4: What's Behind the Win-Lose Mentality? 59

History 60
How it Works 62
Limitations 68

Zero- vs. non-zero sum games	*69*
Conclusion	*70*

Chapter 5: Go Big or Go Home — 73

History and Role in Economics	*75*
How it Works	*78*
Limitations of Decision-Making Games	*84*
Conclusion	*86*

Chapter 6: Forget Your Type. It's All About Guessing Theirs… — 89

History	*92*
How it Works	*94*
Using The Keynesian Beauty Contest In Strategic Voting	*100*
Everyday Applications of the Keynesian Beauty Contest	*102*

Chapter 7: Why Mixing It Up Gives You the Edge — 105

History	*107*
How It Works	*108*
How To Use Mixed Strategies To Get A Higher Pay	*118*
Applying Mixed Strategies to Other Areas of Life	*120*

Chapter 8: What Evolutionary Game Theory Tells Us About Modern Dating — 123

History	*124*

How EGT Can Enhance Your Love Life   *128*
Conclusion   *132*

Chapter 9: A Game Where Everyone Wins (Unless You're a Free Rider)   135

History   *138*
How It Works   *140*
Using Public Goods Games to Organize Parties   *144*
Applying Public Goods Games to Other Areas of Life   *145*

Chapter 10: Navigating Wealth with Game Theory   149

History   *152*
Predicting Competitor Moves with Game Theory Models   *154*
Applying Game Theory to Investment Strategies   *156*
Conclusion   *157*

Takeaways   159

Before You Go…   163

About the Author   165

Reference List   167

Chapter 1: How Game Theory Saved My Life

Smoking was my go-to stress reliever, even though I knew the health risks. In my fifties, my wife didn't mind me smoking half a pack a day because I gave her the same freedom with her nightly glass of wine. It was a win-win: we both had our own little pleasures and respected each other's space. That unspoken agreement was how we kept our marriage strong.

But when we reached our sixties, everything changed. My wife stopped having her nightly drinks, and her concern over my smoking habit became increasingly annoying. She was desperate for me to quit, even going so far as to post sticky notes on my cigarette packs—because, apparently, the government warning wasn't enough. It made sense, though; at our age, the risks of heart disease, lung cancer, and other serious health issues were higher.

However, I was stubborn. I tried to hide my smoking from her, of course, but the scent was too strong to conceal. Frustrated that she couldn't get me to stop, she eventually gave me an ultimatum:

if I didn't quit smoking, she wouldn't sit down for dinner with me anymore. That hit hard. Suddenly, I found myself at a crossroads, weighing my habit against the health of our relationship. I could continue indulging in my vice or choose to prioritize our bond.

That was when I truly understood the stakes. Reevaluating my choices made it clear that some risks just weren't worth taking. When I thought about it, all I really wanted was to live a long life and spend it with my wife. Quitting smoking wouldn't just preserve my health; it would also strengthen our partnership, leading to a more fulfilling life together. Ultimately, that decision saved not just my second marriage, but my life as well.

Funnily enough, it got me thinking about my dad. He was a big smoker when I was a teenager, and if my mom had asked him to quit back in the '70s, it would've been so much harder. Cigarette ads were everywhere, glamorizing smoking and making it seem cool and normal. But things started to change when, on April 1, 1970, Richard Nixon signed the Public Health Cigarette Smoking Act, banning cigarette ads on broadcast media due to rising concerns about the dangers of smoking.[1]

---

[1]Sullivan, M. (2024, March 29). President Nixon signs legislation banning cigarette ads on TV and radio. *HISTORY*

The ban, however, didn't really stop my dad from buying cigarettes. He kept purchasing, just like everyone else. You'd think that without commercials constantly pushing cigarettes, smoking rates would drop, but the opposite happened: profits for tobacco companies actually went up. It seemed counterintuitive at first, but **game theory** helps explain why.

But first, let me define game theory. It's a mathematical branch that studies how and why individuals (called players) make decisions in various situations, especially when their choices affect one another[2]. In the context of the tobacco industry, the players are the major cigarette companies competing for market share. They have to think strategically about how their actions impact not only their own profits but also those of their competitors.

Before the ban, these companies were in a competitive cycle, pouring money into advertising to avoid losing customers to rivals. All companies would have been better off if they could have cooperated and refrained from advertising. However, with the fear that a competitor might gain an advantage, each company felt compelled to

---

.https://www.history.com/this-day-in-history/nixon-signs-legislation-banning-cigarette-ads-on-tv-and-radio

[2]Hayes, A. (2024, June 27). Game Theory: A Comprehensive Guide. Retrieved from https://www.investopedia.com/terms/g/gametheory.asp

advertise, leading to inflated costs without significantly changing sales.

Once the ban was in place, the game changed. No one could advertise on TV, so the companies no longer needed to spend money fighting for airtime. They reallocated those funds to other platforms, like print and billboards, and without the pressure of competing ads, they found a new equilibrium that allowed their profits to rise.[3]

In the end, game theory saved the tobacco companies by helping them adapt to the changing market after the advertising ban. But this strategic thinking isn't just for businesses; it can change the game in our personal lives, too. I shared earlier how it helped save my life (and second marriage). And I'm here to teach you how it can save yours—even in the most awkward situations.

History

Before diving into practical applications, let's take a quick look at where game theory comes from. Game theory gained traction in the 20th century, primarily due to Jon Von Neumann and Oskar Morgenstern. Their 1944 book, *The Theory*

---

[3] Pilat D., & Sekoul D. (2021). Game Theory. The Decision Lab. Retrieved August 19, 2024, from https://thedecisionlab.com/reference-guide/economics/game-theory

of Games and Economic Behaviour, laid the foundation for modern game theory.

Before their contributions, strategic thinking was all over the place. There wasn't a clear framework. Von Neumann and Morgenstern brought the idea that games, where outcomes depend on the decisions of multiple players, could be analyzed in a structured way.

Then came American mathematician John Nash, who built on their work with his concept of Nash equilibrium. In simple terms, a **Nash equilibrium**[4] happens when each player chooses the best strategy based on what everyone else is doing.

If Player A decides to switch things up without considering Player B's moves, they might not get ahead, leading to a balanced outcome. This concept has become a key part of game theory, helping us understand how players can find stable solutions even when their interests don't align. The Nash equilibrium occurs when both players use strategies that benefit them equally.

---

[4]Team, C. (2023, November 22). Nash equilibrium. Retrieved from https://corporatefinanceinstitute.com/resources/economics/nash-equilibrium-game-theory

Key Concepts[5]

To fully understand game theory, you need to learn its language and terminologies. Here's a simple primer to help you follow along with the rest of the book:

- **Player:** The term player usually refers to anyone making strategic decisions in the game. It could be a person, a company, or even a country.

- **Strategy:** A plan or an action that the player follows to win the game.

- **Payoff:** The outcome of executing a strategy successfully or winning the game. It could be a cash prize or even intangible rewards like reputation or satisfaction.

- **Equilibrium**: The point in a game after each player has made a decision and an outcome that benefits both parties is reached.

---

[5]Hayes, A. (2024, June 27). *Game Theory: A Comprehensive guide.* Investopedia. https://www.investopedia.com/terms/g/gametheory.asp#toc-useful-terms-in-game-theory

Types of Games[6]

Game theory has different forms, each with its outcome and strategies, and the common five are listed below:

1. Cooperative and Non-Cooperative Games:

Cooperative games focus on players forming groups to strategize for a collective payoff. Think about a group of cat lovers working on a TNVR (Trap-Neuter-Vaccinate-Return) project to manage stray cats and fairly distribute rewards for their efforts.

In contrast, **non-cooperative games** focus on individual goals. A classic example is the **prisoner's dilemma**, where two people must decide between cooperating or acting in their own self-interest, impacting each other's outcomes. This is similar to the tobacco industry after the 1971 ad ban I mentioned earlier. Before the ban, companies fiercely competed in advertising to keep customers. Once the ban was in place, they redirected their funds elsewhere and ended up increasing profits, showing how competition can shift dramatically.

---

[6] What Are the 5 Types of Game Theory? An In-Depth Look into Applying Them to Your Business. (n.d.). https://gamify.outfieldapp.com/gamification/business/sales/learning/what-are-the-5-types-of-game-theory

2. Zero Sum vs. Non-Zero Sum Games

Zero-sum games have one winner and at least one loser because each player competes for the same outcome. Sports like tennis, poker, finance markets, and politics all belong under this umbrella.

Meanwhile, the payoffs of players in a **non-zero-sum game** do not necessarily add up to a fixed amount. Players can both win or lose at the same time. Business negotiations are a good example of this, as the ideal outcome is for both businesses to benefit.

3. Simultaneous vs. Sequential Games

In **simultaneous games**, players make their decisions at the same time, often without any clue about what the other players are up to. Imagine two closet companies launching marketing campaigns or planning product launches independently; they're in the dark about each other's choices.

On the flip side, **sequential games** are more like chess. Here, players take turns, and each decision affects the next move. It's all about strategy and tactics, trying to outmaneuver your opponent and stay one step ahead.

4. Perfect vs. Imperfect Games

Perfect and imperfect games describe scenarios where the history of any move made is open to both players or hidden from them. An example of a **perfect game** is checkers. Each player sees the entire board and can make plans to hinder their opponent's move.

On the other hand, games like poker involve hiding information from the players, and this is why they're called **imperfect games**. They can only decide based on the cards they were dealt and how well they can bluff. No player has information on what cards the other player holds.

5. Symmetric vs. Asymmetric Games

In **symmetric games**, players have equal opportunities and strategies, leading to balanced competition. For example, in a table tennis match between two evenly matched players, each competitor has similar skills and tactics, making their chances of winning comparable.

Asymmetric games, on the other hand, happen when players have different levels of experience or resources. For instance, if a professional table tennis player competes against a beginner, the professional's advantages significantly shift the dynamics of the match. This also applies to sales strategies, where established market leaders may face new entrants with different resources or tactics, altering the competitive landscape.

Applications of Game Theory

Game theory breaks down any situation where your best move depends on what others do, which is why it's useful in so many areas of life.

- **Economics**

A lot of what companies do comes down to what their competitors are up to—whether it's launching new products, changing prices, or rolling out marketing campaigns. Think about gas stations, for example. You'd think they'd spread out across a neighborhood to cover more ground, right? But instead, they usually bunch up in busy areas. It's because if there's no competition, a gas station can open anywhere it wants. But once others come into play, everyone tries to set up where they can grab the most customers. If a new station opens too far from the pack, it might struggle to get business. That's why they tend to stick close together.[7]

- **Political Science**

In politics, decision-making is often shaped by what opponents are doing, leading to some pretty complex dynamics. Political leaders don't just focus on their own goals—they also have to consider how their rivals might react. A recent

---

[7]Becher, J. (2012, July 27). Why Gas Stations Are So Close To Each Other. Forbes. Retrieved from https://www.forbes.com

study[8] by Ying Chen, an economics professor, used game theory to tackle political gridlock, especially around environmental regulations. She noticed how environmental policies tend to change with each new administration, so she looked into strategies for leaders committed to long-term change. Chen's research suggests that by pushing for innovations that make green options cheaper, politicians can encourage sustainable practices that stick, even as political power shifts.

- **Dating and Relationships**

It is all about how our decisions impact each other. But most of the time, choosing to cooperate—like being kind and committed—leads to better outcomes than acting solely in one's own interest. Just like in any game, what one person does influences the other, making it crucial to consider your partner's actions. By understanding these dynamics, you can navigate the ups and downs of relationships with a bit more insight and strategy.[9]

- **Entertainment**

---

[8]Nitkin, K. (2023, October 6). *A game theory strategy to fight political gridlock.* Arts & Sciences Magazine. https://magazine.krieger.jhu.edu/2023/05/a-game-theory-strategy-to-fight-political-gridlock/

[9]Binazir, A. (2011, November 17). Dating and Game Theory: How to make Better decisions in your love life. *HuffPost.* https://www.huffpost.com/entry/how-to-date-dating-and-ga_b_561152

Game theory shows up in surprising places, like the game show *Jeopardy!* James Holzhauer, a contestant who won $2.4 million, used game theory to craft his strategy. By focusing on high-value questions and making large wagers on Daily Doubles, he maximized his potential payoff while playing against the strategies of his competitors[10]. His success proves how strategic decision-making influenced by game theory can lead to extraordinary outcomes, even in entertainment settings.

- **Animal Behavior**

Even animals interact strategically. For instance, male stickleback fish display bright red underbellies to attract females but aggressively attack anything else red, mistaking it for a rival. In the Canadian wilderness, chickadees alert others to hawks, while some rodents mimic their calls for added survival chances. Green swordtails observe rival fights to determine which opponents to challenge or avoid. These behaviors illustrate how animals unconsciously use game theory principles to maximize their welfare in a competitive environment.[11]

---

[10] Louie, D. (2019, April 25). Is game theory the secret to winning "Jeopardy!"? ABC7 San Francisco. https://abc7news.com/james-holzhauer-jeopardy-on-game/5269190/

[11] *Game Theory in Animal Behavior: Networks Course blog for INFO 2040/CS 2850/Econ 2040/SOC 2090.* (2022,

The Limitations of Game Theory in Practice

Like most things, game theory has its limitations. While it can indeed save lives, it operates on the assumption that everyone plays by the rules of rationality, always pursuing the highest payoff. However, we aren't cold calculators; emotions and biases often influence our choices, and sometimes false information leads to decisions that would perplex a game theorist. For instance, people might choose to cooperate out of fairness or altruism, even when it defies logic.

Things get even trickier when you throw more players into the mix. As interactions grow more complex—like in the chaotic world of global markets—finding that Nash equilibrium can feel like searching for a needle in a haystack. This complexity often makes it tough to apply game theory effectively without oversimplifying the situation.

That's where behavioral game theory comes in. It takes a more holistic view by mixing in insights from psychology and behavioral economics. It recognizes that we often don't stick to the rational script. Take the Ultimatum Game, for

---

September 22).
https://blogs.cornell.edu/info2040/2022/09/22/game-theory-in-animal-behavior/

example: traditional game theory suggests the proposer should offer the bare minimum while the responder should take it. But we know that many people will reject lowball offers out of a sense of fairness, even if it costs them.

So, while simplified models might not capture all the nuances of human behavior, they do resonate with the idea of Occam's Razor—sometimes, the simplest explanation really is the best. These models are easier to work with and less likely to overcomplicate things[12]. In fact, choosing between a straightforward model and a more elaborate game theory approach can sometimes feel like a classic prisoner's dilemma. But more on that in the next chapter.

---

[12]Wijaya, C. Y. (n.d.). Are We Undervaluing Simple Models? - KDnuggets. Retrieved from https://www.kdnuggets.com/are-we-undervaluing-simple-models

Chapter 2: Thinking Like a Smart Prisoner in Times of Crisis

It was a tough time to be a parent in 1999 because of The Columbine shooting in Littleton, Colorado. On April 20th, two students, armed with guns and bombs, opened fire at Columbine High School, killing 15 people and wounding 28 others. I remember sitting on the couch, glued to the TV, feeling sick to my stomach. My son and daughter were around the same age as most of the victims, and even though we weren't from Colorado, the thought of something like that happening at their school felt all too real. I found myself worrying about how to keep them safe and what I could teach them about looking out for themselves if I wasn't around.

And I can only imagine how much worse it must feel for those living in communities with high crime rates, like in New Mexico. According to Forbes, the state holds the highest crime rate in the nation in 2024, with a staggering 7.80 violent crimes per 1,000 residents and a property crime rate of 29.84 per 1,000 residents. For those living there, that means a 1 in 128 chance of becoming a victim of violent crime.[13]

Other states dealt with the heartbreak of mass shootings as well. In 2016, Orlando saw one of the deadliest mass shootings in U.S. history when Omar Mateen opened fire at the Pulse nightclub, an LGBTQ+ venue, killing 49 people. The following year, a gunman took 59 lives at a Las Vegas concert. Despite these tragedies, gun laws across the U.S. actually became more relaxed[14], which just encouraged more citizens to buy guns. According to a 2023 survey, around 40% of U.S. adults live in homes with firearms.[15] But why? What makes Americans buy guns even though they know they're dangerous?

Well, let's try to understand the decision-making behind it by imagining two neighbors, Billy and Daryl, living in New Mexico. With the increasing crime rate in their state, both are

---

[13]Bieber, C., JD. (2024, March 1). States with the worst crime rates. Forbes Advisor. https://www.forbes.com/advisor/legal/criminal-defense/crime-rate-by-state/

[14]Barash, D. (2020, December 30). *The Prisoner's Dilemma = America's Gun Dilemma*. Psychology Today. Retrieved December 30, 2020, from https://www.psychologytoday.com/us/blog/peace-and-war/202012/the-prisoners-dilemma-americas-gun-dilemma

[15]Geiger, A. (2024, July 24). Key facts about Americans and guns. Pew Research Center. https://www.pewresearch.org/short-reads/2024/07/24/key-facts-about-americans-and-guns/

concerned about their safety and must decide whether to buy a gun for protection. Neither neighbor likes the idea of bringing a gun into their home, knowing it could lead to accidental shootings or worse. Yet, the fear of being the only unarmed neighbor while the other is prepared weighs heavily on their minds.

If none of them buys a gun, they benefit from a safer environment. Research shows that guns stored in homes are more frequently associated with fatal or nonfatal accidental shootings, criminal assaults, and suicide attempts than with being used effectively for self-defense.[16]

However, fear and distrust often drive decisions. What if one neighbor buys a gun and the other doesn't? The armed neighbor might feel a temporary sense of security, but the unarmed neighbor would feel increasingly vulnerable, perhaps pressured to buy a gun as well.

If both neighbors ultimately decide to purchase guns, they might each feel safer, but the truth is that their community becomes more dangerous. More guns in a community often means

---

[16] Kellermann, A. L., Somes, G., Rivara, F. P., Lee, R. K., & Banton, J. G. (1998). Injuries and deaths due to firearms in the home. *Journal of Trauma and Acute Care Surgery*, *45*(2), 263–267. https://doi.org/10.1097/00005373-199808000-00010

more gun-related violence, accidents, and deaths, a reality backed by numerous studies.[17]

This situation raises the most important question: Why do these two neighbors, despite knowing that their individual decisions to buy guns could escalate violence and danger in their community, still choose to arm themselves?

The answer lies in a common decision-making trap. Both neighbors are acting out of self-interest, trying to ensure their own safety, but their combined choices lead to a worse outcome for everyone. The problem faced by the two neighbors is what we call the **prisoner's dilemma.**

History

In game theory, the prisoner's dilemma is a decision-making paradox in which two people acting in their own self-interest fail to produce the best solution.[18]

---

[17]Semenza, D. (2022, June 21). *More Guns, More Death: The Fundamental Fact that Supports a Comprehensive Approach to Reducing Gun Violence in America | Rockefeller Institute of Government.* Rockefeller Institute of Government. Retrieved October 19, 2024, from https://rockinst.org/blog/more-guns-more-death-the-fundamental-fact-that-supports-a-comprehensive-approach-to-reducing-gun-violence-in-america/

[18]Team, I. (2024, June 16). What Is the Prisoner's Dilemma and How Does It Work? Retrieved from https://www.investopedia.com/terms/p/prisoners-dilemma.asp

The concept was born in January 1950 when RAND scientists Merrill Flood and Melvin Dresher invited economist Armen Alchian and mathematician John Williams to a hundred-round game. They found that cooperation occurred 60% of the time, contrary to expectations of mutual betrayal at only 14%. Williams's "Tit for Tat" strategy encouraged Alchian to see the value of collaboration, reflecting David Hume's idea of mutual benefit. This also laid the groundwork for John Nash's insights that repeated interactions promote rational strategies, showing that cooperation can thrive in ongoing relationships.[19]

How It Works

The basic structure of the prisoner's dilemma is simple. Imagine it as a one-time game where you and someone else must decide whether to cooperate or act selfishly. If you both cooperate, you both benefit. But if one person acts selfishly while the other cooperates, the selfish person gains more. The catch is, if both choose to act selfishly, neither gets a good outcome. Knowing this, most people choose the selfish option, even though

---

[19] Page, L. (2023, May 5). The true story of the birth of the prisoner's dilemma. *Optimally Irrational*. https://www.optimallyirrational.com/p/the-true-story-of-the-birth-of-the

cooperation would have been the better choice for both.[20]

Now, let's put this into an example with Alice and Tom, who are caught stealing wallets. Normally, this crime would land them each one year in jail. But the police suspect them of a more serious crime—stealing valuable paintings from a museum.

To crack the case, the police offers Alice a deal: if she testifies against Tom for the more serious crime while Tom stays silent, she walks free, and Tom gets eight years. Tom receives the same deal. If neither testifies, they each serve one year, but if both testify, they each serve three years.

At first glance, the best outcome would seem to be for neither to testify, which would lead to one year in jail for each. However, from Alice's perspective, if she stays silent, she risks facing either one year or eight years, depending on Tom's choice. If she testifies, she faces either no jail time or three years. Testifying seems more appealing to her, and the same logic applies to Tom.

Game theory predicts that both rational, self-interested individuals would end up testifying,

---

[20]Holt, C., Johnson, C., & Schmidtz, D. (2015). Prisoner's Dilemma experiments. In *Cambridge University Press eBooks* (pp. 243–264). https://doi.org/10.1017/cbo9781107360174.014

leading to three years in jail for each—a worse outcome compared to mutual silence, but the most likely outcome based on self-interest.

To help you understand this better, let's put the respective penalties in a table below:

Outcome	Tom Cooperates	Tom Defects
Alice Cooperates	1, 1	8, 0
Alice Defects	0, 8	3, 3

The numbers represent years of jail time based on Alice and Tom's decisions to cooperate or defect. If both cooperate, they each get **1** year in prison. If Alice cooperates and Tom defects, Alice gets **8** years while Tom goes free, and vice versa if Alice defects while Tom cooperates. If both defect, they each receive **3** years.

Now, with those incentives in play, there should be no reason not to betray your partner, right? From Alice's point of view, if Tom says nothing, she can either stay silent and do a year in jail (cooperate) or testify and go free (defect). Classic game theory suggests that the smartest choice would be for her to defect. On the other hand, if Tom decides to testify against her, she can either remain silent, serve eight years in jail, or testify against him and do three. Again, the obvious choice would be to do three over eight.

In both cases, whether Tom cooperated with Alice or defected to the prosecution, Alice would have been better off if she had defected and testified. Since Tom faces the same choices, he too would find that defecting is the better option for him.

The paradox of the prisoner's dilemma is this: both robbers can minimize their total jail time if they cooperate and stay silent (two years total). Still, the incentives they each face separately will always drive them to defect and end up doing the maximum jail time between the two, which is six years total.

Bringing our story back to the two neighbors makes the parallels with the prisoner's dilemma clearer. If both neighbors could trust that the other wouldn't buy a gun, they would both benefit from a safer environment. However, the fear that the other might arm themselves drives both to make decisions that ultimately lead to a more dangerous situation. This, of course, is a simplification that only accounts for gun-related domestic tragedies, discounting the aspect of self-defense against external, violent crime.

Also, real-life experiments show that people often cooperate more than this model would lead you to believe. So, we should take the prisoner's dilemma with a grain of salt. Many criminals have an anti-snitching code, meaning they might refuse a deal. Others might stick to their own set of rules and avoid working with the police for personal reasons. Basically, people don't always follow the theories to the letter.

Now, let's move on to a complex version, which is called the **iterated prisoner's dilemma**. In this thought experiment, we assume the prisoners have been in the same situation multiple times. Because of their history with the scenario, they can adjust and strategize based on previous outcomes.[21]

It might appear that the convicts would choose to cooperate if we repeat the scenario. However, that goes against what game theory suggests. Given that there can be no backlash, when they find out how many times the game will replay, they both have an incentive to deflect on the last round. Knowing that the other person will likely defect in the final round, they're both motivated to snitch as the game progresses—essentially leading to the same outcome all the way back to the first round.

---

[21] Halton, C. (2022, June 28). Iterated Prisoner's Dilemma: Definition, Example, Strategies. Retrieved from https://www.investopedia.com/terms/i/iterated-prisoners-dilemma.asp

Real life rarely works that way, though, and criminals are not always easy to predict. What if, before committing the crime, the two criminals had promised not to confess if they were caught? With that agreement in mind, wouldn't it make sense for them to stay silent and only serve one year in jail?[22] The idea of keeping their word could be strong enough to override the temptation to betray each other, especially if they genuinely want to avoid extra jail time.

But then again, they're both criminals, so how much can you really trust a promise between them? Once they're separated, it's only natural for self-preservation to kick in, and the urge to save themselves often leads to a confession.

What if the game had infinite or random iterations? How would cooperation strategies change? If the prisoners were part of a gang and knew they'd be interacting with each other in the future (either in the same prison or in the outside world), they're more likely to cooperate and stay silent. In that case, the motivation to stick together would be strong. If snitching could lead to a serious beating or even death, the fear of those consequences would make them think twice. With loyalty on the line, they might decide that staying

---

[22]*Prisoner's Dilemma: What Game Are you Playing?* (2020, February 22). Farnam Street. https://fs.blog/prisoners-dilemma/

silent is the better choice, realizing that their safety and future depend on it.

Surviving The Next Pandemic with Prisoner's Dilemma

You and I know that 2020 was rough. The COVID-19 pandemic hit, and it felt like the world just pressed pause. Jobs were lost, hospitals were overwhelmed, and our mental health suffered. Life changed for nearly everyone in ways we never imagined—some lives were altered forever, while others came to an end. As of April 13, 2024, over 7 million people have lost their lives to the virus.[23]

When you think about it, the pandemic was one big prisoner's dilemma.[24] We all had to make tough choices—whether to prioritize our comfort or make sacrifices for the greater good. The pandemic forced us to balance personal needs against community welfare in ways we'd never experienced before.

It was this very concept that inspired researchers like Madhur Anand and Chris Bauch to

---

[23] *COVID-19 deaths | WHO COVID-19 dashboard.* (n.d.). Datadot. https://data.who.int/dashboards/covid19/deaths?n=o

[24] Kaushik, P. (2020, March 17). Covid-19 and the Prisoner's Dilemma. *Asia Times.* https://asiatimes.com/2020/03/covid-19-and-the-prisoners-dilemma/

use game theory to understand why people made the decisions they did. They aimed to answer questions like Who should get vaccinated first to save the most lives? How do personal choices about mask-wearing or social distancing impact the bigger picture?

One of the key insights from their research was that unlike what game theory often assumes—that people always act rationally—many of our decisions were driven by fear, anxiety, and misinformation. These emotions made it harder for people to follow public health guidelines and ultimately hindered efforts to control the virus. When people acted in their self-interest—like avoiding masks or skipping the vaccine—it might have felt easier at the moment, but it often made things worse for everyone in the long run.[25]

If you're reading this book, it means you survived like many others. Whether you fully cooperated or struggled to follow the rules, we all faced difficult choices based on our different situations. I didn't like wearing facemasks because it made me uncomfortable, but I couldn't risk my family's health.

---

[25] Jentsch, P., Anand, M., & Bauch, C. T. (2020). Prioritising COVID-19 vaccination in changing social and epidemiological landscapes. *medRxiv (Cold Spring Harbor Laboratory)*. https://doi.org/10.1101/2020.09.25.20201889

The pandemic forced us to balance self-interest with the greater good, proving how interconnected our actions are and how individual choices shape collective outcomes. Now that we're past it, the real question is: How can we respond better to the next crisis? While I don't want to be pessimistic, it's a possibility we have to consider.

If there's something we learned from COVID-19, it is that cooperation is often the best solution. Communities that cooperated—staying home, wearing masks, getting vaccinated, and embracing new technologies—helped end lockdowns sooner. Still, we must also acknowledge that cooperation can be challenging, especially for those who are not as financially secure as others.

Let's say it's 2050, and two yoga instructors, Julia and Agatha, are facing the COVID-50 lockdown. Julia is financially secure, having enough savings to comfortably stay home and follow all the lockdown rules without worrying about income. On the other hand, Agatha lives paycheck to paycheck without any savings to fall back on. The strict lockdown means she can't hold in-person yoga classes, and online attendance is insufficient to cover living expenses.

Aside from being yoga instructors, Julia and Agatha share the experience of living through the 2020 pandemic, giving them a unique advantage. Even if they don't know each other personally, both understand that cooperation is key. Julia, being financially secure, is likely to follow the rules and could support others by collaborating with less privileged instructors to share income. Cooperation is more challenging for Agatha due to her financial situation, but she can still follow the guidelines while seeking community support or finding ways to engage students online safely.

Surviving the next pandemic will depend on prioritizing the collective good over individual gain. Acting solely out of self-interest leads to multiplying negative consequences, but when we cooperate—by sharing resources, supporting vulnerable people, and following public health measures—we create the best outcomes for everyone.

Solving The Prisoner's Dilemma In Everyday Life

The prisoner's dilemma pops up all the time—whether in your relationships, at work, or even on a larger societal level. It's all about juggling what's best for you with what benefits everyone else, and finding that balance can make life a lot smoother. Here are some smart, real-life ways to deal with it:

- **Build Trust in Relationships**

Trust is the foundation for any relationship. Being upfront and honest with your partner, friends, or family helps avoid drama and keeps things running smoothly. Just like in the workplace where regular check-ins prevent office tension, having open conversations with the people close to you builds a level of trust that encourages everyone to work together. It's like putting deposits in a relationship bank—over time, you've built something solid.

- **Set the Rules in the Workplace**

When you're in a work environment, cooperation often happens through contracts and agreements. Everyone knows what's expected, and there's less room for selfish behavior. Clear guidelines make sure no one is taking advantage. If things go sideways, a mediator or third party can step in and keep everyone in line. It's like setting the rules to keep everyone's interests aligned.

- **Sweeten the Deal in Community and Society**

On a larger scale, people need a little extra push to do the right thing. When you make it more rewarding to cooperate, like offering bonuses for teamwork or penalizing companies for polluting, people are more likely to come together for the greater good. It's all about changing the payoff: when cooperation becomes the winning move, everyone benefits.

As we close this chapter, remember that our social interactions often reflect the prisoner's dilemma, where we balance self-interest with cooperation. However, the **Nash equilibrium** offers a different perspective: it shows how people make decisions based on what they think others will do, leading to a stable outcome where no one has a reason to change their strategy. In the next chapter, we'll discuss how this concept applies to real-life events.

Chapter 3: A Beautiful Blunder

I was in my mid-40s when I first saw *A Beautiful Mind* and, let me tell you, I was completely drawn in by the story of John Nash—a genius wrestling with his own mind. At that age, the film's mix of brilliance and struggle really hit home. But as I've dug deeper into game theory, I've come to see just how far the movie strays from the true heart of Nash's work, especially regarding his concept of Nash equilibrium.

Take that iconic bar scene, for instance. In the bar scene, Nash and his mathematician friends are gathered when a group of women strolls in, featuring one blonde and several brunettes. Although they are all smitten with the blonde, they realize that pairing with a brunette is preferable to being left alone. Nash explains that if all the men pursue the blonde, they risk collective rejection, as she would likely turn them away alongside her friends. While this moment attempts to showcase strategic thinking, it oversimplifies the complexities of Nash equilibrium.[26]

---

[26] J. Rogers (2018 April 27) "The Game Theory Glitch in A Beautiful Mind," *Law & Liberty*, Essay from https://lawliberty.org/the-game-theory-glitch-in-a-beautiful-mind/.

To truly grasp **Nash equilibrium**, it's necessary to first discuss the concept of **Best Response (BR)**. A Best Response refers to the strategy that maximizes a player's payoff given the actions of others. Best example? Think of driving! If one driver decides to go left, the best move for another driver to avoid a collision is also to go left. This means the benefit from a chosen action has to be equal to or greater than any alternatives, based on what others are up to.

Nash equilibrium itself refers to a scenario in which no player can improve their outcome by changing their strategy unilaterally, as each choice is optimal relative to the others. This concept includes pure strategy Nash Equilibria and mixed strategy Nash Equilibria, the latter introducing randomness to strategies, as seen in situations like football penalty shootouts, where both kicker and goalie must avoid predictability to gain an advantage.[27]

Now, back to the bar scene. Nash explains that if the four mathematicians go after the blonde, they could end up blocking each other's chances. Instead, by approaching her friends, they increase their odds of success without conflict. This

---

[27] "Mukund" (2021 January 17). "A Beautiful Theory: A Beautiful Mind—Understanding Nash equilibrium." Article from https://reachoutmukund.medium.com/a-beautiful-theory-a-beautiful-mind-understanding-nash-equilibrium-f7646e9dfda1.

illustrates the assumptions underlying Nash equilibrium, where collective interests can lead to more favorable outcomes. While the film captures the idea that individuals must consider the actions of others in their decisions, it overlooks the broader implications of Nash equilibrium for understanding human interactions across various contexts, which I will explore further in the following sections.

So, was the film a HIT or a MISS? Regardless of where we stand, we have to appreciate the valuable lessons Nash's theories provide. They offer profound insights into how we navigate our interactions in life and work, extending well beyond the film's portrayal. Ultimately, this film leaves us with important lessons—if we take the time to truly understand Nash equilibrium, we can apply its principles to enhance our own decision-making and interactions.

History

Nash equilibrium, discovered by American mathematician John Nash, is one of the most influential concepts in game theory. Picture a busy intersection where drivers must decide whether to stop at a red light or run it. But here's the twist—what if that light's out? Now, it's up to each driver to decide: stop or go? This is where things get interesting, as each driver's choice depends not only on their own preferences but also on what they expect other drivers to do. Welcome to the crossroads of the Nash equilibrium. [28]

    Let's break it down. Say there are two drivers at the intersection. If they both stop, sure, there's a small delay, but nothing major—let's call it a -3 each. Now, if they both decide to go at the same time, we're talking about a mess—a collision, with a serious cost of -20 for both. But if one driver stops and the other goes, the one who goes gets through smoothly with a payoff of +5, while the one who waits just has to sit tight for a moment, taking a small hit at -1.[29]

---

[28]Majumdar, M. (2018, March 8). How Nash equilibrium applies in traffic signals. Retrieved from https://www.linkedin.com/pulse/how-nash-equilibrium-applies-traffic-signals-mrittika-majumdar/

[29]Cornell University (2022 November 2). "Crossing an Intersection and Nash equilibrium." Blog post from https://blogs.cornell.edu/info2040/2022/11/02/crossing-an-intersection-and-nash-equilibrium

		Driver 2's Decision	
		Driver 2 Stop	Driver 2 Go
Driver 1's Decision	Driver 1 Stop	(-3, -3)	(5, -1)
	Driver 1 Go	(-1, 5)	(-20, -20)

[30]

So, what's the smart move here? According to this concept, the best play is to let one person go while the other waits. Both sides are better off, and no one's dealing with a wreck or a repair bill. It's that balance—knowing how your decision fits with everyone else's—that keeps life moving along without too many bumps. And that, my friend, is Nash equilibrium in action.

The Nash equilibrium describes a state where the game reaches its best possible result.[31] This equilibrium is stable if no player has a unilateral incentive to deviate from their chosen strategy. When all players announce their strategies simultaneously, they have no desire to change their

---

[30]*Image created by Author*

[31]Chen, J. (2024 June 5). "Nash equilibrium." Investopedia. https://www.investopedia.com/terms/n/nash-equilibrium.asp.

decisions, which highlights the concept's significance, particularly in economics, due to its versatile interpretations.

Strategies outside the equilibrium generally lead to poorer results. But following equilibrium strategies keeps each player's choice aligned optimally with the others, ensuring the best possible outcomes for all. In predictive contexts, Nash equilibrium acts as a stable point within a dynamic adjustment process, where players refine their strategies based on the response to others. This principle has broad applications, extending from economics to biology, where mixed strategies can reflect population dynamics.

Additionally, Nash equilibrium functions as a self-enforcing agreement, aligning the self-interests of players and distinguishing between cooperative and noncooperative games.[32] In his seminal 1950 paper, Nash defined this equilibrium and proved its existence using Kakutani's fixed-point theorem, establishing a foundation for contemporary economic analysis. His groundbreaking work, along with contributions from John Harsanyi and Reinhard Selten, earned him the Nobel Prize in 1994, highlighting the

---

[32] Holt, C. A., & Roth, A. E. (2004 March 15). "The Nash equilibrium and market design." Proceedings of the National Academy of Sciences, 101(47), 16820-16825. Research article from https://www.pnas.org/doi/10.1073/pnas.0308738101.

concept's extensive implications across diverse fields.[33]

How it Works

In a Nash equilibrium, each player selects the strategy that maximizes their expected payoff based on the strategies chosen by others. In the realm of two-player matrix games, this equilibrium signifies that each player's choice is optimal when considering the other's decision. Understanding this concept is crucial, as it applies to various real-world scenarios where individuals or entities must make strategic choices.

The Prisoner's Dilemma is a common situation analyzed in game theory that can employ the Nash equilibrium. We touched on this in an earlier chapter, so let's jog your memory.

	Confess	Stay silent
Confess	(-10, -10)	(0, -20)
Stay silent	(-20, 0)	(-1, -1)

[34]

---

[33] Harsanyi, J. (1967–68) *Manage. Sci.* 14, 159–182, 320–334, 486–502.

[34] *Image created by* Social Sciences LibreTexts. Retrieved from

As illustrated above, if one player decides to confess, the other player is better off also confessing to avoid a worse outcome. Specifically, if the row player confesses, the column player also chooses to confess because a payoff of -10 is preferable to -20. This mutual confession leads to a Nash equilibrium because neither player has an incentive to change their strategy unilaterally.[35]

Let's consider a more relatable example. Suppose my wife and I are trying to coordinate when to watch our favorite TV series, given our schedules. If I get home first and she's late, I waste time waiting for the show to start. Conversely, if she arrives first and I'm late, she ends up sitting there alone, missing the excitement. The Nash equilibrium in this situation arises when we both arrive early, allowing us to enjoy the show together, or if we both decide to work late, making more money and to binge-watch later. These two scenarios illustrate the Nash equilibria.[36]

---

https://socialsci.libretexts.org/Bookshelves/Economics/Introduction_to_Economic_Analysis/16%3A_Games_and_Strategic_Behavior/16.02%3A_Nash_Equilibrium

[35] Introduction to Economic Analysis." (n.d.). "Games and Strategic Behavior: Nash equilibrium." LibreTexts. https://socialsci.libretexts.org/Bookshelves/Economics/Introduction_to_Economic_Analysis/16%3A_Games_and_Strategic_Behavior/16.02%3A_Nash_Equilibrium.

[36] Quora Contributor. (2014 July 16). "Nash equilibrium Explained." Quora. https://www.quora.com/Nash-Equilibrium-Explained.

	I go home	I work late
She goes home	(3, 3)	(1, 2)
She works late	(2, 1)	(2, 2)

Finally, it's worth noting that many folks mistakenly think a dominant strategy is just the same as a Nash equilibrium. But let me tell you, that's not the case. A dominant strategy can lead to a Nash equilibrium, but the two concepts aren't interchangeable.

A dominant strategy occurs when players make their best choices without considering what others do—each player acts independently.

In contrast, Nash equilibrium happens when players factor in each other's strategies and make informed decisions based on that knowledge. While a dominant strategy can sometimes result in a Nash equilibrium, the reverse is not true.[37]

---

[37] Majaski, C. (2023 August 13). "What's the Difference Between a Dominant Strategy Solution and a Nash equilibrium Solution?" Investopedia. https://www.investopedia.com/ask/answers/071515/what-difference-between-dominant-strategy-solution-and-nash-equilibrium-solution.asp.

Limitations

Nash equilibrium has been used in various fields, like psychology, political science, and economics, to predict human behavior. It helps explain many situations, such as why countries engage in nuclear arms races and why businesses compete fiercely. However, it's important to remember that Nash equilibrium has its limitations. It doesn't always capture the complexity of human behavior or the nuances of certain situations.

- **Assumes rationality**

Like many game theory ideas, Nash equilibrium relies on the idea that every player in a game is rational and will always choose their own course of action based on the information at hand. In reality, though, this isn't always the case. People frequently make decisions not in their best interests due to emotional influence or other considerations.[38]

Take the Ultimatum Game, for instance. In this scenario, one player proposes a division of a sum of money, and the second player can either accept or reject the offer. If accepted, both players receive

---

[38]Faster Capital. (n.d). *The Limitations of Nash equilibrium*. Retrieved from https://fastercapital.com/topics/the-limitations-of-nash-equilibrium.html.

their shares; if rejected, they both get nothing.[39] The Nash equilibrium suggests that the second player should accept any offer greater than zero since it's better than getting nothing. However, in reality, many individuals turn down offers they perceive as unfair or outright insulting, even if it means walking away with nothing.

Imagine if you got $1 offered out of $10. Would you be happy with your dollar, knowing that the other scrooge gets $9 – when they could have chosen to give you $5, say? Or would you find some satisfaction in the fact that neither of you gains anything?

- **Assumes everyone has the same information**:

In real-world scenarios, players often lack complete knowledge about their game. Since Nash equilibrium assumes that everyone has perfect information, they know every aspect of the game, including the other players' plans and payoffs. However, players' decision-making is impacted since they frequently get inaccurate or partial information.[40]

---

[39]"Ultimatum Game." Wikipedia, The Free Encyclopedia. https://en.wikipedia.org/wiki/Ultimatum_game.
[40]Faster Capital. (n.d). *The Limitations of Nash equilibrium*. Retrieved from https://fastercapital.com/topics/the-limitations-of-nash-equilibrium.html.

Take **poker**, for example. In this game, players must make decisions based on limited information about their opponents' cards and strategies. Each player's knowledge about the other players' hands is hidden, which directly influences their strategy and potential outcomes.

In competitive situations like games, auctions, or military operations, the strategies and desired outcomes of opponents are often unknown. This lack of transparency makes Nash equilibrium less effective as an analysis method in real-world competition.[41]

- **Only occurs in finite games**

Nash equilibrium is applicable only in finite games, where a limited number of player actions exist. Consequently, it cannot be applied to situations that lack clear endpoints or winners, such as ongoing business competitions or historical and political scenarios.[42]

---

[41] Kingston, M. (2023 September 12) *"Understanding Nash equilibrium in Game Theory."* https://builtin.com/data-science/nash-equilibrium.

[42] *Ibid.*

Case Study and Significance of Nash Equilibrium

A great example of Nash equilibrium is the pricing strategies of competing businesses, such as two competing coffee shops, Coffee Shop A and Coffee Shop B, situated on the same street. Both establishments are vying for a shared customer base, with the option to set their coffee prices at $3, $4, or $5. The customer demographics consist of 20 locals, who consistently choose the shop with the lowest price, and 40 tourists, who select randomly between the two cafes.[43]

	B $3	B $4	B $5
$3	$90, $90	$120, $80	$120, $100
$4	$80, $120	$120, $120	$160, $100
$5	$100, $120	$100, $160	$150, $150

---

[43] *Ibid.*

To analyze this situation, we can use a payoff matrix. The matrix displays the potential revenue outcomes for each coffee shop based on the price they choose:

In this matrix, the first number represents the revenue for Coffee Shop A, while the second number indicates the revenue for Coffee Shop B. Each coffee shop aims to maximize its revenue, considering the pricing strategy of the competitor.

Nash equilibrium occurs when neither coffee shop has an incentive to change its pricing strategy, given the pricing of the other. For example, if both A and B set their prices at $4 (resulting in payoffs of 120 for both), neither would gain any advantage from altering their price.

If A were to lower its price to $3 while B remained at $4, A might attract more customers, but this would come at lower revenue per sale. But if B increased its price to $5, it might lose customers to A, negatively impacting its overall revenue.

Importantly, multiple Nash equilibria exist in this scenario (highlighted in red). If both coffee shops maintain the same price, an equilibrium is reached.

The significance of Nash equilibrium in this case study extends far beyond theoretical applications.

1. **Nash's Existence Theorem** guarantees at least one equilibrium in finite games, such as pricing strategies for coffee shops. This principle is essential for owners seeking reliable pricing methods in competitive markets.

2. **Computational Elegance** highlights the straightforward nature of Nash equilibrium analysis, makes it accessible for evaluating competitive strategies, allowing quick assessments of potential outcomes and enhancing strategic planning.

3. **Multiple Equilibria** present an opportunity for deeper insights but also complicate decision-making. Coffee shops must consider various pricing scenarios to determine optimal strategies, which can be challenging when multiple equilibria exist. Owners need to weigh the potential benefits of different pricing strategies against the risks of competitors altering their prices in response.[44]

Ultimately, understanding Nash equilibrium promotes a proactive approach to decision-making, highlighting the interconnectedness of choices in both business and personal contexts.

---

[44] *Ibid.*

Chapter 4: What's Behind the Win-Lose Mentality?

All over the globe, billions went about their daily lives with no knowledge of how the decisions of a few men would steer the course of history. The year was 1945, and the location was the Potsdam Conference. The most powerful leaders of the era gathered to make a choice that would influence the trajectory of global history post-World War II. The atmosphere in the room was tense, as every move on the geopolitical chessboard could shift the scales of power.

The leaders present understood that every decision they made would alter the global landscape, with gains for one side meaning losses for another. It was a textbook case of a zero-sum game—key topics included the division of Germany, territorial claims in Eastern Europe, and reparations, with Stalin aggressively seeking to expand Soviet influence.

Harry S. Truman, newly sworn in as President of the United States, recognized the monumental stakes of the negotiations. He possessed a decisive advantage: knowledge of the atomic bomb, which could either bring a swift end to the conflict or ignite future tensions. This weapon had the potential to shift the global power landscape dramatically. As the leaders negotiated, Stalin aimed to solidify his power in Eastern Europe, understanding that any concession from the Allies would enhance his position.[45]

The decisions made at Potsdam not only concluded World War II, but also laid the groundwork for the Cold War, reshaping international relations for years to come.

History

The term "zero-sum" originated in game theory during the 1940s and represents a fundamental concept where the gains and losses of all participants are exactly balanced. In such games, the total change in wealth or benefit remains zero. When one player secures a win, another experiences an equivalent loss, resulting in a net total that sums to zero.

A practical example of a zero-sum game is poker. In poker, the amount won by the winning player equals the combined losses of the losing players, making it a classic zero-sum game.

---

[45]McDonough, J. (2021, May 14). Berlin Experiences. The Potsdam Conference: July 23rd, 1945 - Koenigsberg, Prussia. Retrieved from https://berlinexperiences.com/the-potsdam-conference-july-23rd-1945-koenigsberg-prussia/

Similarly, if there is one winner and one loser in most games or contests, i.e. tennis, chess, arm wrestling, or dominoes—it qualifies as a zero-sum game.[46]

Historically, zero-sum games have been central to numerous negotiations and conflict resolution, and competitions. Apart from the Potsdam Conference, which shaped the post-WWII World order, several other notable examples come to mind:

1. **The Punic Wars (264–146 BC)**: The series of wars between Rome and Carthage ended with Rome controlling the western Mediterranean and Carthage's destruction, illustrating a clear zero-sum outcome.

2. **The Cold War (1947–1991)**: The U.S. and Soviet Union viewed gains in the space race or military expansion as losses for the other, reinforcing the zero-sum mindset throughout their political and military rivalry.

3. **The Treaty of Tordesillas (1494)**: Spain and Portugal's division of new lands was a zero-sum game, with Spain claiming most of the Americas

---

[46]Market Business News. (n.d.). *Zero-sum game: Definition and meaning*. Retrieved from https://marketbusinessnews.com/financial-glossary/zero-sum-game-definition-meaning/

while Portugal gained Eastern territories and trade routes.

4. **The Game of Chess**: A literal example of a zero-sum game, where two players compete for control of the board. Each move that captures a piece or strengthens one's position directly weakens the opponent's standing.[47]

Yet, zero-sum games aren't just historical relics. They still appear in various areas today, which will be explored in the following sections. These dynamics remain relevant in many aspects of life, and we'll dive into how they play out in the next parts.

How it Works

Game theory identifies three potential outcomes in a game or financial interaction: win-win, zero-sum, and lose-lose situations. A **zero-sum situation** occurs when one party's gain is exactly balanced by another party's loss. For example, if two friends, A and B, bet on a football game, one friend's win results in the other's loss, leading to no net change in overall points. The concept of zero-sum games originated from the

---

[47]Faster Capital. (2024 June 19). *Zero-sum game: Winning at all costs – Dominant strategies in zero-sum scenarios*. Retrieved from https://www.fastercapital.com/content/Zero-Sum-Game--Winning-at-All-Costs--Dominant-Strategies-in-Zero-Sum-Scenarios.html#Introduction-to-Zero-Sum-Games

idea that one party's loss corresponds directly to another's profit, which helps maintain balance within the financial system.

As our economic understanding evolved, it became evident that one participant does not have to incur a loss for another to gain. Situations can exist where all parties benefit, known as win-win scenarios. Conversely, there are instances where all parties may experience losses, resulting in a lose-lose outcome.

In a zero-sum situation, the surrounding environment must treat all participants equally. Resources cannot be adjusted according to individual needs, meaning the total profits and losses must balance out to reflect a fair game.[48]

Consider a retired individual deciding whether to use a $2,000 windfall to travel or invest in a local community project. If the decision is made to spend that money on a vacation, it may seem that the community project is the loser. Yet, investing in the project could yield benefits down the line, fostering community development and potentially enhancing the individual's quality of life through greater social connections.

---

[48] Pathak, S. (2024 August 21.). *Zero-sum game*. Wall Street Mojo. Blog from https://www.wallstreetmojo.com/zero-sum-game/

Conversely, if the money is dedicated to the community project, it may appear that the individual is forgoing a personal experience. However, the long-term gains, such as improved community resources and increased property values, could outweigh the immediate pleasure of travel.[49]

The Cambridge Dictionary defines a zero-sum game as *"a situation in which an advantage that is won by one of two sides is lost by the other."*[50] In competitive settings like investing or community engagement, a well-thought-out strategy and informed decision-making are essential for achieving the desired outcomes.

- Stock Markets

In financial markets, trading futures exemplifies zero-sum games, as for every dollar spent, there is a dollar gained and vice versa. In these scenarios, participants are speculators who bet on the future prices of assets or commodities. For instance, if a trader suspects that the price of a futures contract will fall, they may start buying it. When the price rises as predicted, they can sell the commodity at the agreed price before the contract

---

[49]Market Business News. (n.d.). *Zero-sum game: Definition and meaning.* Retrieved from https://marketbusinessnews.com/financial-glossary/zero-sum-game-definition-meaning/

[50] Cambridge Dictionary. (n.d.). *Zero-sum game.* https://dictionary.cambridge.org/dictionary/english/zero-sum-game

expires, realizing a gain. Meanwhile, another trader who pays more for the same product at that time incurs a loss. Thus, the net change in profit or loss is zero, illustrating the zero-sum situation.

In contrast, stock market trading does not fit this model; the interaction between buyers and sellers can lead to gains or losses that do not necessarily balance out to zero, as stock prices fluctuate based on market conditions.[51]

For example, Forex, stocks, or futures trading in the financial markets are all zero-sum. Any profit you make from the market comes at the expense of another's loss. This same concept applies to business competition, where companies vie for market share.

- Trade & Bargain

Zero-sum thinking often emerges in trade negotiations and social politics, where one side's gain is perceived as another's loss. For example, in trade negotiations, countries might worry that lowering tariffs will weaken them. However, both sides can benefit from finding common ground, like working together on technology or environmental projects.

---

[51]Pathak, S. (2024 August 21.). *Zero-sum game*. Wall Street Mojo. Blog from https://www.wallstreetmojo.com/zero-sum-game/

In economic terms, an increase in demand for a product raises its price, while a decrease leads to a price drop. In international trade, the success of one country often seems to come at the expense of another. The global economy operates as a complex web of zero-sum games, where one region's gain frequently hinges on another's setback.

Similarly, in social politics, disputes over resources can foster a zero-sum mentality. However, everyone can win by finding creative solutions, like expanding budgets or shifting funds. By understanding each other's needs and looking for shared benefits, what seems like a conflict can turn into cooperation.[52]

- Psychology

Zero-sum thinking appeals to our logical instincts: when I win, you lose. It's one of the simplest ways to understand competition, but it can also be limiting. While this perspective simplifies competition, it can also limit our ability to recognize opportunities for cooperation and mutual benefit. When we perceive every interaction as a conflict between adversaries, we risk overlooking solutions that could serve everyone's interests. Understanding the zero-sum bias is crucial, as it can

---

[52]Faster Capital. (2024 June 19). *Zero-sum game: Winning at all costs – Dominant strategies in zero-sum scenarios*. Retrieved from https://www.fastercapital.com/content/Zero-Sum-Game--Winning-at-All-Costs--Dominant-Strategies-in-Zero-Sum-Scenarios.html#Introduction-to-Zero-Sum-Games

significantly influence decision-making and behavior across various contexts.

This bias is sometimes amplified by individuals seeking to gain an advantage. Some politicians, for example, bolster their support by convincing the public that resources are limited and must be fought over. They often invoke the lump of labor fallacy, suggesting there's a fixed number of jobs. In their view, bringing new folks into the job market must come at the expense of those already employed.

The implications of zero-sum thinking extend beyond social dynamics. Consumer behavior, too, is impacted. They may mistakenly assume that if a product excels in one area, it must fall short in another, believing that positive attributes must be offset by negative ones. For example, if a phone is known for its durability, consumers might expect it to lack performance. Similarly, this bias can shape career choices, leading individuals to believe that higher salaries correlate with poorer work-life balance. It also influences various aspects of decision-making, such as evaluating evidence and seeking information.[53]

---

[53] Effectiviology. (n.d.). *Zero-sum bias*. Retrieved from https://effectiviology.com/zero-sum-bias/#Dangers_of_the_zero-sum_bias

Limitations

In modern economics, not every competition follows a zero-sum structure. There are many situations where all parties can benefit. Take the classical (Ricardian) theory of trade, for instance, which argues that all nations involved in trade can benefit simultaneously. In these cases, competition doesn't have to mean someone's loss for another's gain.[54]

However, it is crucial to recognize that not all trades result in positive outcomes. If one player suffers an injury and another chooses to retire rather than accept a trade, both teams may face losses, leading to a net negative result. Unlike zero-sum games, where one party's gain corresponds directly to another's loss, non-zero-sum games can yield both positive and negative results.

---

[54]Market Business News. (n.d.). *Zero-sum game: Definition and meaning.* Retrieved from https://marketbusinessnews.com/financial-glossary/zero-sum-game-definition-meaning/

Zero- vs. non-zero sum games

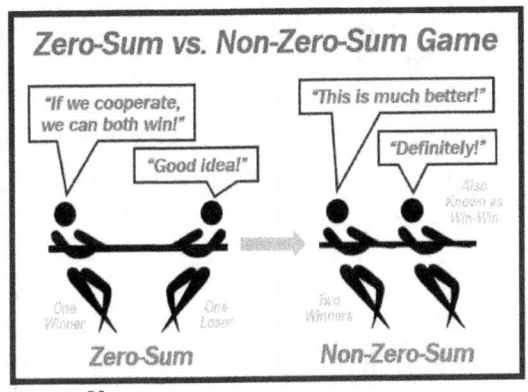

Understanding strategic interactions requires a clear distinction between zero-sum and non-zero-sum games. Not every interaction is a straightforward contest where one party wins and another loses. Non-zero-sum games offer a different perspective, where both parties have the potential to benefit. Consider the scenario of two sports teams engaged in a trade; if each team addresses a pressing need, the result can be a mutually advantageous arrangement. [56]

---

[55] *Image created by Market Business News.* Retrieved from https://marketbusinessnews.com/financial-glossary/zero-sum-game-definition-meaning/

[56] Market Business News. (n.d.). *Zero-sum game: Definition and meaning.* Retrieved from https://marketbusinessnews.com/financial-glossary/zero-sum-game-definition-meaning/

Conclusion

Zero-sum games should be approached with caution. The winner-take-all mentality fosters an unhealthy, competitive environment where individuals prioritize winning over their true objectives. This approach can stifle collaboration and hinder long-term progress.

Moreover, it assumes that success is binary, that you can either win or lose. Success is, however, more complicated, with numerous shades of gray. A company could have an excellent year even if it isn't the market leader. Narrow definitions of success can be deceptive, and zero-sum games fail to account for this important subtlety.[57]

The appeal of zero-sum thinking lies in its simplicity—it's straightforward to believe that one person's gain must come at another's expense. Yet, in today's intricate world, this perspective can hinder our ability to recognize opportunities for collaboration and mutual growth. By fostering a mindset that values win-win outcomes, we can enhance our interactions across business, politics, and personal relationships. In an era marked by

---

[57] Faster Capital. (2024 June 19). *Zero-sum game: Winning at all costs – Dominant strategies in zero-sum scenarios*. Retrieved from https://www.fastercapital.com/content/Zero-Sum-Game--Winning-at-All-Costs--Dominant-Strategies-in-Zero-Sum-Scenarios.html#Introduction-to-Zero-Sum-Games

interdependence, seeking mutually beneficial arrangements not only enriches our endeavors, but also lays the groundwork for a more sustainable path to success.

Chapter 5: Go Big or Go Home

Growing up in the South meant sweltering days and simple entertainment, often capped off by a trip to the local cinema. Not until the year of 2007, the television landscape underwent a significant upheaval during the Writers Guild of America (WGA) strike. This event not only disrupted production schedules but also led to substantial financial losses for both writers and studios, with the L.A. economy estimated to lose between $75 and $100 million due to the cancellation of the Golden Globes. Much like in the Ultimatum Game, the strike became a vivid example of how the entertainment industry had turned into a battleground for negotiations.[58]

The Ultimatum Game is a fundamental experiment in economic and psychological research, how individuals make decisions based on fairness rather than purely rational calculations. In this scenario, it involves two players: a proposer and a responder. The proposer is given a certain amount and must decide how much to offer the

---

[58]The Writer's Strike and Game Theory. James D. Miller. 04 Jan 2008. Web.

responder, who starts with nothing. The game's outcome rests on the responder's reaction: if the offer is accepted, both players keep their shares. However, if the offer is rejected, both lose everything.[59]

During the strike, each side attempted to gain negotiation leverage by deceiving the other about their true beliefs. Each side aimed to demonstrate their willingness to reject any solutions or proposals they deemed unjust, even if such actions seemed counterproductive.[60] Perceptions of fairness and trust significantly influence outcomes, underscoring that the fight for equity often trumps short-term gains.[61]

In response, the writers used arguments considered socialist to rally their supporters around lofty objectives, such as a war on labor. However, given their comfort within a capitalist system, their commitment to socialism seemed insincere. If their claims had been more genuine, they might have gained greater leverage.

---

[59] iMotions. (n.d.). The ultimatum game: Theory, variations, and implications. Retrieved from https://imotions.com/blog/learning/research-fundamentals/the-ultimatum-game/

[60] Miller, *The writer's strike and game theory*.

[61] iMotions. (n.d.). The ultimatum game: Theory, variations, and implications. Retrieved from https://imotions.com/blog/learning/research-fundamentals/the-ultimatum-game/

So, are you curious about who came out on top of this negotiation? Me too! According to a New York Times article, both parties took a hard line and had to compromise. While both sides sacrificed short-term profits from traditional distribution, writers secured a more substantial cut of future digital revenues.[62]

History and Role in Economics

The Ultimatum Game developed by Güth, Schmittberger, and Schwarze in 1982 examines how people handle monetary offers and fairness. In this game, a proposer decides how to split a sum of money, while a responder can accept or reject the offer. [63]

Unlike the Dictator Game, which we will discuss in the next sections, the Ultimatum Game allows responders to reject offers. If the offer is rejected, both players walk away with nothing. Such rejections indicate negative reciprocity (Rabin, 1993)—the desire to punish unfair treatment—or inequity aversion (Fehr and Schmidt, 1999), reflecting a distaste for unfair

---

[62] Carr, D. (2008, February 12). Who Won the Writers Strike? *The New York Times*. Retrieved from https://www.nytimes.com/2008/02/12/arts/television/12strike.html

[63] Houser, D., & McCabe, K. (2014, Pages 19-34). "Ultimatum Games." In *Neuroeconomics* (Second Edition pp. 19-34). https://www.sciencedirect.com/topics/neuroscience/ultimatum-game.

outcomes. Typically, offers below 20% are rejected about half the time, prompting proposers to average around 40%. Cross-cultural studies suggest that in societies where cooperation and market trade are common, ultimatum offers tend to be more generous (Henrich et al., 2001).[64]

What's truly striking is that many people will reject unfair offers, even at a personal loss. This behavior challenges the classic economic view that we're purely self-interested.[65] The Ultimatum Game introduces us to experimental economics, highlighting that we're not just rational decision-makers. Traditional economics often assumes this, but real-world experiments consistently shake up these long-held beliefs. It's a straightforward point, and especially relevant today as more people are encouraged to take control of their financial futures.[66]

Recent research using social exchange paradigms illustrates a significant shift in

---

[64]Fehr, E., & Krajbich, I. (2014). "Ultimatum Games." In *Neuroeconomics* (Second Edition, pp. 193-218). https://www.sciencedirect.com/topics/neuroscience/ultimatum-game.

[65]Houser, D., & McCabe, K. (2014, Pages 19-34). "Ultimatum Games." In *Neuroeconomics* (Second Edition pp. 19-34). https://www.sciencedirect.com/topics/neuroscience/ultimatum-game.

[66]Starmer, C. (2014, July 18). "Nudge novelty has worn off, but we still need behavioural economics." *The Conversation*. https://theconversation.com/nudge-novelty-has-worn-off-but-we-still-need-behavioural-economics-29514.

understanding human behavior within economic contexts, refining traditional economic models. Researchers are moving beyond simple bargaining over a "gift." One approach involves delaying rewards, which requires participants to decide how to split waiting times (Berger et al., 2012), while other studies focus on sharing workloads, such as solving mathematical problems (Ciampaglia et al., 2014). These findings reveal that individual contributions create "entitlements" that significantly influence proposed offers. For example, individuals designated as dictators in Dictator Games tend to give less if they've earned that right compared to when the endowment is randomly assigned (Hoffman et al., 1994; Cherry et al., 2002). Additionally, in one adaptation of the Ultimatum Game, responders who generate their own endowments increase their offers, suggesting that cooperative behavior stems from the source of entitlement (Carr and Mellizo, 2013).[67]

However, let's not ignore how behavioral economics is viewed today. We often present it through straightforward examples, which can lead some critics to argue it lacks depth. While the formal models of behavioral economics sometimes

---

[67] Bland, A. R., Roiser, J. P., Mehta, M. A., Schei, T., Sahakian, B. J., Robbins, R. W., & Elliott, R. (2017, June 16). "Cooperative Behavior in the Ultimatum Game and Prisoner's Dilemma Depends on Players' Contributions." *Frontiers in Psychology*.
https://www.frontiersin.org/journals/psychology/articles/10.3389/fpsyg.2017.01017/full

spring from simple insights, they can be even more complex than traditional economic models. As Einstein quipped, "Elegance is for tailors." [68]

Despite its complexity, behavioral economics offers a treasure trove of insights. Some concepts might be trickier than the clear-cut lessons of the Ultimatum Game, but we must remember that grappling with these complexities is crucial for truly understanding decision-making in all its forms.

How it Works

Let's say you are a subject in a university study. The researcher gives you $10 and asks you to split it with another participant. You could decide to keep $7 for yourself and offer $3 to the other person. If they agree, both of you get your share as planned. But if they reject it, neither of you receives anything, and the money is lost.

In summary, if the other party agrees to the suggestion, the money is distributed accordingly. However, if the other participant refuses the division, neither party receives anything. [69]

---

[68] Starmer, C. (2014, July 18). "Nudge novelty has worn off, but we still need behavioural economics." *The Conversation*. https://theconversation.com/nudge-novelty-has-worn-off-but-we-still-need-behavioural-economics-29514.

[69] McHugh, L. (n.d.). *Chapter 10: Game theory and strategic decision making*. McGraw-Hill Education. Retrieved from

If we decide to visualize the Ultimatum Game, it unfolds like this:

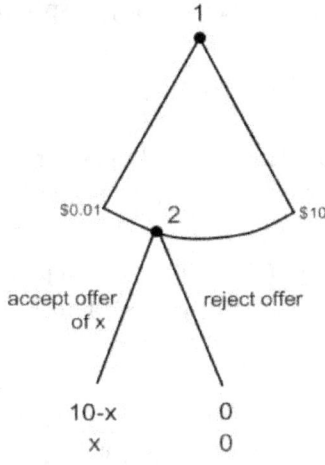

The rules of the game:

Player 1: Receives an amount (usually $10) and must propose how to split it between themselves and Player 2. The offer can be any amount from $0.01 to the full $10.

---

https://highered.mheducation.com/sites/dl/free/0077108310/329284/CH10.pdf

[70] *Image created by Presh Talwalkar.* Retrieved from https://mindyourdecisions.com/blog/2015/10/13/this-is-your-ultimatum-game-this-is-your-ultimatum-game-on-drugs-game-theory-tuesdays/

Player 2: Can either accept or reject Player 1's offer.

- **If accepted**: The money is split according to Player 1's offer.
- **If rejected**: Both players receive nothing.

Strategic reasoning: Behind this game, it's helpful to use a concept called "reverse induction," starting from the end result. If Player 2 is solely motivated by money, participants should accept any offer—no matter how small—because receiving something is better than nothing.

- **Player 1's leverage**: Knowing Player 2 won't walk away empty-handed, Player 1 can offer the smallest penny (e.g., $0.01) and keep the majority for themselves, thereby maximizing their own gain.

Power dynamic: This is why the game is called the "ultimatum game." Player 1 holds the power of negotiation: to issue a "take it or leave it" offer, and Player 2 will accept, driven by the rational desire to gain something, even if it's unfair.[71]

Concepts:

---

[71]CORE Econ. (n.d.). Strategic interactions: The ultimatum game. Retrieved from https://www.core-econ.org/the-economy/microeconomics/04-strategic-interactions-11-ultimatum-game.html

- **The Pursuit of Self-Interest**

Veronica generally takes a fancy briefcase with her when she goes out of town on business. One day, a stranger notices it and, thinking her an economist, assumes she's self-interested and reasonable. This assumption leads the thief to consider stealing her briefcase. However, he wonders if he can escape punishment, given that the cost of filing charges might exceed the briefcase's value.[72]

If Veronica's briefcase is stolen and she chooses to press charges, then she'll most likely miss her flight home. Not only would she have to return to testify at the trial, but she'd also face the possibility of being subjected to a tough cross-examination by the thief's attorneys. Given these associated costs, it seems logical for Veronica to write off the loss of her briefcase. Although she could have deterred the thief by threatening to press charges, that threat holds little weight because the thief understands the cost-benefit analysis favors his decision to steal.

This scenario highlights how individuals make decisions based on perceived self-interest, similar to players in the ultimatum game who gauge how their offers will be received.

---

[72]Talwalkar, P. (n.d.). *The joy of game theory*. Book. Retrieved from https://pdfcoffee.com/presh-talwalkar-the-joy-of-game-theory-pdf-free.html

- Market (Dynamics and Incentives)

A successful business owner, let's call him Calvin, wants to open a new branch in a distant city. If he employs someone to manage the new office, he can pay a $1,000 weekly compensation (a $500 increase above what the manager could typically earn). This arrangement also allows Calvin to earn a weekly profit of $1,000 for himself. He is worried about one thing, grappling with a significant concern about how to oversee the manager's actions effectively.

Calvin understands that this manager could, through unscrupulous means, increase his take-home income to $1,500 by running the remote office fraudulently, which would ultimately cost him $500 every week. With these drawbacks in mind, should Calvin consider opening the new office if he thinks all managers are self-serving money-maximizers? [73]

The decision tree for the remote office game is shown below.

---

[73] *Ibid.*

Decision	Outcome	Owner's Payoff	Manager's Payoff
A: Calvin opens a new branch	Manager behaves honestly	$1,000	$1,000
	Manager behaves dishonestly	-$500	$1,500
B: Calvin doesn't open a new branch	No manager	$0	-

At option A, Calvin decides whether to open a new branch. The manager faces a choice between honesty and dishonesty. Should the manager act with integrity, both she and Calvin benefit, earning $1,000 each. However, if she opts for dishonest practices, Calvin incurs a loss of $500, while she walks away with $1,500. At option B, if Calvin decides not to open a new branch, no manager is involved, and the owner earns $0, which is better than a $500 loss.

In the end, the opportunity cost of the manager's inability to make a credible promise is $1,500: the manager's forgone $500 salary premium and the $1,000 return Calvin stands to lose.

Calvin's approach exemplifies the intricate nature of decision-making in business, where trust and the potential for self-serving behavior play crucial roles. His dilemma resonates with the core principles of the ultimatum game, highlighting that while profit is a primary concern, understanding human behavior and the dynamics of trust are equally vital for sustainable success.

Limitations of Decision-Making Games

The Dictator Game is a modified form of the Ultimatum Game. In this experimental setup, one individual (the dictator) is given an endowment and decides how much to give to a random, anonymous recipient. Unlike in the Ultimatum Game, if the recipient finds the offer undesirable, they cannot penalize the dictator. Instead, they accept whatever amount is offered.[74]

In traditional economic theory, it's expected that the "proposer" will offer the smallest amount possible to maximize their own gain, and the "responder" will accept any non-zero offer, as something is better than nothing. However, real-world experiments like the Ultimatum Game tell a different story.

---

[74] Ahlstrom, L. (2023, August 30). Ultimatum game. *INOMICS*. Retrieved from https://inomics.com/terms/ultimatum-game-1538668

Proposers tend to offer around 40 to 50 percent of the total sum, significantly more than the theoretical minimum. In comparison, responders often reject offers below 30 percent of the total, even if it means walking away with nothing. This behavior contradicts the principles of economic self-interest, as rejecting an offer leads to a loss. Yet, fairness, revenge, and a desire to punish perceived injustices often outweigh pure financial gain.[75] Much like the WGA strike, it wasn't just about the money—it was about perceived fairness. Writers and studios both risked immediate losses, hoping to achieve a more equitable share in the long run.

In contrast, conventional economic theory suggests that, in a dictatorship, participants would offer nothing because there would be no repercussions. Yet, results of trials using Ultimatum Games show that when social distance between parties narrows, dictators tend to act more charitably. The tendency to contribute a non-zero portion of the endowment suggests that individuals, particularly in organizations, may consider concepts of justice and charity in addition to self-interest when making decisions. Members of an organization may behave more kindly when there is less social gap between them, which would improve the organization's welfare and results.

---

[75] CORE Econ, *Strategic interactions: The ultimatum game*.

Research on Dictator Game experiments reveals that details about the recipient can significantly influence how much a dictator offers. Brañas-Garza (2006) studied the conduct of dictators under three distinct information scenarios.

1. **No Information**: In the absence of recipient details, 71% of dictators made no donation, with an average contribution of only 10% of the endowment.

2. **Recipient's Poverty**: When informed that the recipients were impoverished and from developing nations where the funds could be useful, 46% of dictators donated their entire endowment, while 22% chose not to contribute at all.

Medications vs. Cash: After learning that the recipients were impoverished and that donations would be made in the form of medications rather than cash, 72% of dictators donated the full amount, averaging 65% of the endowment.[76]

Conclusion

The implications of the Ultimatum Game extend beyond economics, influencing the very

---

[76]Brañas-Garza, P. (2006, July 31). Poverty in Dictator Games: Awakening solidarity. *Journal of*

nature of our social interactions. Choices made by proposers and responders reflect a fundamental human instinct for fairness, even at a personal cost. This instinct shapes negotiations in various contexts, be it in the boardroom, at the bargaining table, or in daily life.

Consider, for instance, Veronica and her encounter with a potential thief. As the thief weighs the legal risks against the value of her briefcase, we see how individuals navigate the delicate balance between self-interest and fairness. Similarly, Calvin's decision to open a new branch emphasizes this dynamic, forcing him to evaluate profit potential against the integrity of his manager. If she chooses honesty, both can prosper; if she opts for dishonesty, Calvin stands to lose significantly. These scenarios illustrate how negotiation choices reflect deeper social instincts, underscoring the critical importance of trust and fairness.

In examining the parallels to the Ultimatum Game, we understand that effective negotiation requires more than simply securing the best deal. It demands a thoughtful balance of trust, fairness, and strategic thinking. Ultimately, the lessons from both the game and the WGA strike remind us to reassess our approaches to negotiation. The pursuit of equity often outweighs short-term financial gains, leading to more fruitful and harmonious interactions in both professional and personal contexts.

As we move forward to the next chapter, we'll explore the Keynesian beauty contest. Just to clarify, I'm not referring to a type of pageant show.

Chapter 6: Forget Your Type. It's All About Guessing Theirs...

Ever find yourself nodding along to something you don't even like just to keep the peace? We've all been there. A decade ago, I was out with colleagues after a rough day, and what started as a pizza debate quickly got tense. I was all in on mushrooms and onions, but as everyone exchanged tired glances, I could feel the pressure. No one wanted to argue anymore. Then came the question: "What are we ordering?" I went with pepperoni—not because I wanted it, but because I thought *everyone else* did.

It's funny how often we make choices not based on what we actually want but on what we think *others* want. This goes beyond small decisions, like picking a pizza or a movie. It seeps into bigger areas of life where we start playing a subtle guessing game, trying to anticipate what others will choose or prefer instead of following our instincts. In doing so, we often forget that everyone else might be doing the same thing—choosing what they think others expect rather than what they truly want.

This kind of thinking behavior was explored in 2011 by NPR's Planet Money podcast through a fascinating experiment. They asked listeners to pick the cutest animal from three videos, but with a twist. The 12,000 participants were divided into two groups: one was asked to pick the cutest animal based on their opinion, and the other group had to choose the animal they believed everyone else would think was the cutest. The choices were a slow loris, a baby polar bear, and a kitten.[77]

In the first group, about half picked the kitten. No surprises there. Interestingly, in the second group, 76% chose the kitten—even though many admitted it wasn't the cutest in their eyes. Take Marla Woods, one of the participants, for instance. She actually preferred the slow loris, but she still picked the kitten because she believed most people would. However, here's the catch: when we keep choosing something just because we think everyone else will, we end up with overvaluation—a phenomenon the podcast called a "kitten bubble."

But here's the thing about bubbles—they're fragile. A bubble bursts when the underlying value doesn't match the hype. In the "kitten bubble," if people realized they didn't really think the kitten

---

[77]Npr. (2011, January 12). Our cute animal experiment, explained. NPR.
https://www.npr.org/sections/money/2011/01/11/132838904/the-tuesday-podcast-our-cute-animal-experiment-explained

was the cutest and stopped choosing it just because others did, the whole inflated perception would collapse. Everyone starts to question their assumptions, and suddenly, the kitten wasn't as popular as it seemed.

This is exactly what happens in financial bubbles. Remember NFTs? NFTs, or "Non-fungible tokens," were all the rage in 2021. People weren't buying them because they truly understood their value, but because they believed others would pay even more for them. As more people jumped on the bandwagon, prices soared. But when the excitement died down and people started realizing that the actual value didn't match the hype, the NFT bubble began to deflate. It was fueled by speculation and crowd mentality, and once that illusion broke, the inflated prices came crashing down.

This type of decision-making isn't new. It actually ties back to a concept introduced by economist John Maynard Keynes, known as the **Keynesian Beauty Contest**. In this game, contestants didn't pick the person they thought was most beautiful; instead, they chose who they believed everyone else would select. The further you go into this kind of second-guessing, the more it shifts from opinion to pure strategy. It becomes less about what you think and more about trying to predict the choices of others.

In a way, trying to predict market trends is a lot like guessing who your friend will end up with—it's easy to misjudge. Just as we often get it wrong when we try to guess our friends' preferences, the Keynesian Beauty Contest shows how easy it is to make poor decisions when we focus too much on anticipating others' choices.[78]

History

In the 1930s, there was a popular newspaper game where readers were asked to choose the most beautiful faces from 100 images. Each reader had to choose six faces, and their choices were then compared to the selections of other participants. A player would win a prize if their selections matched the most popular faces chosen by the majority.

John Maynard Keynes, the famous British economist, came across this game in his local newspaper one morning. Despite being a brilliant macroeconomist, Keynes often struggled in the stock market. He knew more about macroeconomics than most of Britain and tried to use this knowledge to predict shifts in financial markets based on macroeconomic policies.

---

[78]Research Video: The economic engineer comes to the Keynesian Beauty. (2021, August 30). Retrieved from https://bse.eu/news/research-video-economic-engineer-comes-keynesian-beauty-contest

However, that approach rarely worked, and he often ended up with only average returns. [79]

After struggling to do so consistently, Keynes began to question whether it was even possible to predict the market. He became interested in developing a model to explain the rapid stock market bubbles, crashes, and other price swings even when basic value remained unchanged. The beauty contest game piqued his interest as a potential model for this, and he wrote about it in his 1936 book, *The General Theory of Employment, Interest, and Money*.

Keynes pointed out that there are several strategies one could use when participating in a beauty contest game. One way, according to economists, is called a "naive strategy."[80] Basically, it is when you simply choose the faces you think are the prettiest, assuming everyone else will think the same way. But most people aren't doing that—they're actually trying to guess what *others* will pick. The really strategic players? They go even further, trying to guess what everyone else is guessing others will pick.

---

[79] The Keynesian Beauty Contest - the Decision Lab. (n.d.). Retrieved from https://thedecisionlab.com/reference-guide/psychology/the-keynesian-beauty-contest

[80] BusinessDay. (2021, November 11). *Playing the Keynesian beauty contest game on the NSE - Businessday NG*. Businessday NG. https://businessday.ng/analysis/article/playing-the-keynesian-beauty-contest-game-on-the-nse/

How it Works

A simple way to demonstrate the concept is through the original beauty contest game.[81] In the game, participants are asked to pick a number between 0 and 100, and the winner is the person who selects the number closest to two-thirds (2/3) of the average of all the numbers chosen by participants.

At first glance, it might seem straightforward to pick a random number. However, it gets more complicated once participants realize they need to think about what others will pick. If everyone picks higher numbers, the average will be high, and two-thirds of that will still be a sizable number. But if participants anticipate that others will think this way and pick lower numbers, they need to adjust their guesses accordingly.

This is where the **2/3 rule** comes in: instead of simply picking a number based on your own preference, you're trying to guess what two-thirds of the average will be, which requires predicting others' choices.[82]

---

[81] Mauersberger, F., & Nagel, R. (2018). Levels of Reasoning in Keynesian beauty Contests: A Generative framework. In *Handbook of computational economics* (pp. 541–634). https://doi.org/10.1016/bs.hescom.2018.05.002

[82] Nsut, I. G. T. S. (2021, December 9). Keynesian Beauty Contest - The Indian Game Theory Society, NSUT - Medium. Medium. Retrieved from https://medium.com

Now, Keynes explains that different levels of thinking come into play. I'll give you some context now, and I'll explain more later:

- **Level-0 (Zeroeth-level thinkers)**: These are the *naive* players. They don't consider what others might do and make their choice based purely on their own instinct or preferences.
- **Level-1 thinkers**: These players think strategically for the first time. They assume the Level-0 players are acting naively and try to make a choice based on what they expect those players to do.
- **Level-2 thinkers**: These players think one step further. They anticipate what the Level-1 thinkers will do and adjust their own choice based on that expectation.
- **Level-3 thinkers**: These are the more advanced strategists. They think about what the Level-2 thinkers are likely to do and respond accordingly, trying to stay one step ahead in their reasoning process.

If everyone thinks at the highest level of rationality, the Nash equilibrium would be 0 since 2/3 of 0 is 0. However, in reality, people don't always think that far ahead, so the winning number is often somewhere between 10 and 20, depending on the group's overall level of thinking.

		Group Average		
		50	**33**	**22**
Choices	Player 1	33	22	15
	Player 2	22	15	10
	Player 3	15	10	7

This matrix above shows how each player's choice affects the average and the 2/3 rule. As players think more deeply, their numbers approach the final winning range.

Now, let's break down the thought process for each level of thinker:

- A Level-0 thinker would assume the average to be around 50, leading them to choose something close to 50.
- A Level-1 thinker would take things a step further, realizing that the average of the zeroth-order choices is around 50. So, they calculate that 2/3 of that would be roughly 33, and they choose accordingly.
- A Level-2 thinker goes even deeper, anticipating that most participants will be

first-order thinkers who select 33. They will then pick 2/3 of 33, which is around 22, thinking they've outwitted the others.
- Every level of reasoning that comes after aims to outguess the one before, resulting in guesses that decrease progressively.

The Keynesian Beauty Contest is less of a guessing game and more of a prediction game, where success depends on anticipating the collective behavior of everyone else. And it isn't just a thought experiment. It happens daily in real-world markets, where investors constantly try to predict what others will do.

A great example of the Keynesian Beauty Contest in action is Amazon. For years, Amazon wasn't turning huge profits, yet investors kept buying shares. They believed in its long-term potential, sure, but they also figured others would catch on and drive the stock price up. So even when Amazon wasn't raking in big profits, its stock price kept soaring because people were betting on future growth—and, more importantly, betting that everyone else would be too.

Back in the late 1990s, tech stocks were booming as everyone rushed to pour money into internet companies. But people weren't buying these stocks because of their actual value—they were buying because they expected others to push the prices even higher. Of course, the dot-com bubble eventually burst in 2000, and a lot of investors were left with some pretty heavy losses.[83]

Bitcoin and other cryptocurrencies are modern examples of this same behavior. A lot of people aren't investing because they believe in the actual value of Bitcoin, but because they think others will keep pushing the price higher. It's a speculative game where everyone's trying to guess what the next person will do, which is why it's so volatile and prone to bubbles.

Tesla's stock price is another example. It's often driven more by market hype than by traditional valuation metrics. Investors have pushed Tesla's price to sky-high levels, not necessarily because of its current performance but based on what they think others will believe about Tesla's future. This leads to constant swings in price, driven by crowd psychology rather than cold, hard data.

Both examples reflect how crowd behavior shapes markets, and they tie into another important concept in behavioral economics: **bounded rationality**. This refers to the idea that people don't always make fully rational decisions because

---

[83]International Banker. (2021, September 29). *The Dotcom Bubble Burst (2000)*. https://internationalbanker.com/history-of-financial-crises/the-dotcom-bubble-burst-2000/

they're constrained by limited time, information, and cognitive ability. In the numbers game, some players stop at the first or second level of thinking while others dig deeper. In real markets, the same limitations apply—investors don't always have perfect information or unlimited time to make the best possible decision. Instead, they work within their limits, and that's what creates the unpredictable and often volatile behavior we see.

Similarly, investors often rely on heuristics, or mental shortcuts, to make decisions in real-world markets. Instead of diving into every detail of a stock's value, they might go with trends, the latest news, or just gut feelings. These shortcuts can lead to unpredictable outcomes, much like in the numbers game, where different levels of reasoning produce a range of guesses and results.

After experiencing some early losses in his investment career, Keynes realized that trying to outguess others in financial markets was a risky gamble. He changed his approach to **value investing**, where the focus is on finding stocks that are undervalued based on their actual potential—not just what others think about them.

This long-term strategy was later popularized by investors like Warren Buffett, who famously said: "Be fearful when others are greedy, and greedy when others are fearful." Instead of constantly trying to predict the market's next move, value investors zero in on an asset's real worth and hold onto it until the market catches up. This shift in thinking helped Keynes consistently outperform the market, and it's now considered one of the most successful investing principles.

Using The Keynesian Beauty Contest In Strategic Voting

Believe it or not, this same logic from The Keynesian Beauty Contest can help you make smarter political decisions.

Let's say it's election day, and two friends, Sarah and Drew, are at the polls. Sarah's heart belongs to Candidate A, but she knows deep down they don't stand much of a chance. Drew prefers Candidate C but has noticed that Candidate B is leading in the surveys and still aligns with some of his values. They're both facing a classic voting dilemma: vote for the candidate they love, or vote with their heads, trying to outguess how others will vote?

Sarah sticks with her gut, voting for Candidate A. But Drew casts his vote for Candidate B. Why? Because he thinks beyond his personal preference and tries to predict how the majority will vote. He wants his vote to count for a candidate with a realistic chance of winning.

Drew's decision-making captures the essence of **strategic voting**[84]—it's not just about personal preference, but about making a calculated choice based on predicting the bigger picture. In essence, Drew, like participants in a Keynesian Beauty Contest, tries to second-guess the preferences of the larger voting body, not unlike picking the 'average opinion' that Keynes described.

Research shows that some voters rely on strategic thinking more than others. People who excel at **strategic inference**[85], or predicting what others will do, are more likely to base their decisions on a candidate's chances of winning rather than just personal preference.

The closer the race, the more vital strategic thinking becomes. Studies by Blais and Nadeau (1996) and Abramson et al. (1992) reveal that when elections are tight, voters are far more likely to abandon their top choice in favor of a candidate with a better shot at winning.[86] Just like in a Keynesian Beauty Contest, where the winner is the

---

[84] *The many faces of strategic voting : tactical behavior in electoral systems around the world.* (2018). The Library of Congress. https://www.loc.gov/item/2018055286

[85] Loewen, P. J., Hinton, K., & Sheffer, L. (2015). Beauty contests and strategic voting. *Electoral Studies*, *38*, 38–45. https://doi.org/10.1016/j.electstud.2015.01.001

[86] Blais, A., & Nadeau, R. (1996). Measuring strategic voting: A two-step procedure. *Electoral Studies*, *15*(1), 39–52. https://doi.org/10.1016/0261-3794(94)00014-x

one who predicts the average choice of others, strategic voting hinges on reading the room—or, in this case, the polls.

So, before you cast your vote, consider the broader field. If the race is close, you might want to back a candidate who isn't your top pick but stands a better chance. Like Drew, you're shaping the outcome by thinking beyond your personal favorite, ensuring your vote contributes to a result that still reflects your values.

When enough voters act strategically, they can shift outcomes that shape policies, societal values, and even global relations. It's not just about personal preference anymore—your vote becomes part of a larger game where individual choices collectively steer the future for the better.

Everyday Applications of the Keynesian Beauty Contest

The idea behind the Keynesian Beauty Contest shows up in so many other parts of life, where decision-making is all about predicting what others will do. Whether it's in business, job interviews, or even social situations, being able to anticipate what others might choose can give you a real advantage in getting the outcome you want.

- **Marketing**

    When launching a product or service, don't just stick to your own preferences—think about what will resonate with your audience. Just like in a Keynesian Beauty Contest, success comes from predicting the crowd's favorite, not your own. For example, in fashion, if you're designing a new clothing line, you might love bold, avant-garde styles, but if consumer trends lean toward minimalism, you're better off aligning with that trend to maximize sales.

- **Job Market and Career Choices**

    In the job market, career decisions are often made based on how you think others—like employers—will evaluate your qualifications. Instead of just focusing on what *you* want, consider the trends and demands in your industry. For instance, if you're a software engineer deciding between learning blockchain development or web design, you might choose blockchain not because you love it more, but because you predict a higher demand for blockchain experts in the future.

- **Social Dynamics and Relationships**

    In social situations, it's not just about saying what's on your mind—you also have to anticipate how others will react. For instance, if you're in a group discussion and you notice that certain opinions are getting more positive feedback, you might adjust your argument or tone to fit the group's vibe. Similarly, in dating, you might pick up on subtle cues to predict your date's preferences—maybe they seem adventurous eaters, so you suggest a Somali restaurant, even if that's not your first choice.

As we wrap up the beauty contest of second-guessing and crowd predictions, it's tempting to think we've got the strategy game all figured out. But sometimes, the smartest move isn't just about predicting others—it's about adding a twist to your own play.

What happens when sticking to just one approach isn't enough? That's where we're headed next. Let's just say the next game gets a little more… unpredictable.

Chapter 7: Why Mixing It Up Gives You the Edge

As kids, one of the first games we learned was called "hide and seek." If you're reading this and enjoying retirement like me, allow me to remind you of the rules: one person covers their eyes and counts while everyone else scatters to find *that* perfect hiding spot. Not to toot my own horn, but back in the day, I was never the seeker. In my seven-year-old mind, all I knew was I must avoid being found at all costs. I remember having this little trick which I never told anyone, thinking it was the sole reason why I was a genius in the game. It was simply reminding myself, "Never hide in the same spot!"

As I grew older and my hair thinned out, I realized that my favorite childhood game wasn't just about hiding and finding; it really was a kid-friendly introduction to strategy. It turns out that my "little trick" wasn't just a random thought; it was a subconscious effort to be unpredictable. I was purposely making a way to not be easily found by changing my hiding spot every single time. Why? Well, let's just say I loved keeping the seeker guessing.

But this instinct for unpredictability isn't just powerful during playtime. It's fascinating to learn that long before I ever thought of my own tactics, Napoleon Bonaparte was doing a similar thing to win the Battle of Austerlitz[87] in December 1805.

His epic move wasn't a straightforward attack, but a clever deception to make the Russian troops believe he was weaker than he actually was. He deliberately weakened his right flank, pulling back some of his forces and creating the illusion of vulnerability.

This tactic led the Russians to believe it was the right time to attack, completely unaware that Napoleon had lured them toward the frozen lake. Once the Russians were finally in a vulnerable position, Napoleon seized the opportunity, unleashing his concealed reserves to attack their enemies at their center, resulting in their downfall.

Just as I switched up my hiding spots during hide and seek, Napoleon mixed up his tactics in battle. He injected deception into his plans, making it tough for anyone to figure out his true intentions. For instance, he might have alternated between

---

[87]Lehmann, J. (2024) *The Battle of Austerlitz and the utility of game theory for operational analysis*, *E*. Available at: https://www.e-ir.info/2024/04/09/the-battle-of-austerlitz-the-utility-of-game-theory-for-operational-analysis/

retreating and fortifying positions, thereby keeping the enemies uncertain about his next move.

History

In game theory, what I did back then (and what Napoleon did masterfully) has a name: **mixed strategies.** A mixed strategy[88], first coined by economic professors Douglas Bernheim and Michael Whinston in 2005, is a decision-making approach where a player randomizes their choices instead of consistently doing the same action[89].

The importance of using mixed strategies is well-documented in numerous undergraduate economics texts. According to economists Robert Pindyck and Daniel Rubinfeld, certain games do not favor a pure strategy, suggesting that relying solely on a single approach may not produce optimal results. This indicates the need to incorporate a mix of strategies.

Author and economics professor Roger McCain also points out that unpredictability is essential for players, as it prevents opponents from

---

[88] Blackwell, D. et al. (1996) Statistics, probability, and game theory: Papers in honor of David Blackwell. Ithaca, NY, Durham, NC: Cornell University Library ; Duke University Press.

[89] Garrett, K., & Moore, E. (2008). Teaching Mixed Strategy Nash equilibrium to undergraduates. *International Review of Economics Education*, 7(2), 79–87. https://doi.org/10.1016/s1477-3880(15)30088-8

accurately anticipating their moves. This idea is further supported by Bernheim and Whinston, who argue that success in strategic interactions hinges on maintaining an element of unpredictability, advocating for random decision-making to gain the upper hand.

The significance of mixed strategies is also emphasized in the book *Mathematical Economics*, which asserts that not all games feature pure strategy Nash equilibria, where players consistently choose a single approach. In many economic scenarios, solutions are only attainable through mixed strategy, where players randomize their choices by establishing the probabilities of selecting different pure strategies.

How It Works

Let me explain this concept through a classic example. Imagine two players, Kelsey and Jacob, playing a game called Matching Pennies. The mechanics are simple: Kelsey and Jacob each have a penny. They have to flip their coins secretly, choosing either heads or tails. They reveal their choices at the same time. If their pennies match (both heads or both tails), Kelsey wins and gets both pennies. If they don't match (one heads and one tails), Jacob wins and gets both pennies.

Of course, if Kelsey wants to win, she must guess what Jacob will do. If she thinks he'll flip heads, she'll choose heads too, hoping they match. Jacob is trying to outsmart her by choosing the opposite side to win. Let's break it down with a payoff table:

		Jacob	
		Heads (H)	Tails (T)
Kelsey	Heads (H)	(1, -1)	(-1, 1)
	Tails (T)	(-1, 1)	(1, -1)

In this game, the values of 1 and -1 in the table illustrate a straightforward win-loss scenario. A value of 1 indicates a win for the player, meaning they gain the pennies, while -1 signifies a loss, indicating that the player loses the pennies. For instance, if Kelsey goes for Heads (H) and Jacob also chooses Heads (H), Kelsey wins, leading to a payoff of (1, -1).

Conversely, if Kelsey chooses Heads (H) while Jacob selects Tails (T), Jacob wins, resulting in a payoff of (-1, 1). Similarly, when Kelsey picks Tails (T) and Jacob chooses Heads (H), Jacob once again comes out on top, with a payoff of (-1, 1).

Lastly, if both Kelsey and Jacob select Tails (T), Kelsey wins, which produces a payoff of (1, -1).

Instead of always picking heads or always picking tails, Kelsey and Jacob decide to mix up their strategies. Kelsey might choose heads 50% of the time and tails 50% of the time. This way, Jacob can't predict what she'll do. Jacob does the same, mixing his choices to keep Kelsey guessing.

The example demonstrates the importance of strategy, unpredictability, and the use of mixed strategies in competitive situations, showcasing how both players can adapt and respond to each other's moves effectively.

But you might be wondering, is there a time when "unpredictability" is not the answer? Well, before we dive into that, let's explore this next example, which I'm sure you're already familiar with - Rock-Paper-Scissors.

In this classic game, each player selects one of three moves: rock, paper, or scissors. The interactions are simple yet strategic; rock crushes scissors, scissors cut paper, and paper covers rock. If we stick to the basic principle of mixed strategies—where you vary your moves every single time—you're likely to experience the three outcomes over the course of your lifetime: win (1), lose (-1), or draw (0):

	Rock	Paper	Scissors
Rock	0,0	-1,1	1,-1
Paper	1,-1	0,0	-1,1
Scissors	-1,1	1,-1	0,0

If you're a competitive player, you'll be delighted to know that there is a way to increase your chances of winning. Recent research by Zhijian Wang and his team at Zhejiang University has revealed that real players don't actually play completely randomly. While it makes sense to assume that mixing it up is the best strategy, the findings indicate that players actually use predictable patterns[90].

Their experiments with 360 students showed that while players generally chose each action about one-third of the time (as expected in random play), closer analysis unveiled repeating moves. Winning players tended to repeat their moves (Rock → Rock → Rock), while losing players shifted to the next action in a clockwise direction (Rock → Paper → Scissors).

---

[90]arXiv, E.T. from the (2024) How to win at Rock-paper-scissors, MIT Technology Review. Available at: https://www.technologyreview.com/2014/04/30/13423/how-to-win-at-rock-paper-scissors/

This behavior aligns with psychological principles beyond game theory—people tend to stick with strategies that have worked for them, reinforcing their winning moves. This reliance on past successes makes games more predictable, allowing smart opponents to exploit these patterns.

While the traditional advice to "mix it up" aims to keep opponents guessing, being somewhat predictable can actually be advantageous. Recognizing and utilizing these natural patterns—like continuing a winning move—can give you an edge. Sometimes, incorporating predictability into your strategy can have better results. In short, being predictable can be an unpredictable move, too. How mind-blowing is that?

When Mixed Strategies Are Not the Only Way.

Aside from being two simple games, Matching Pennies and Rock-Paper-Scissors have something else in common: they do not have pure-strategy Nash equilibrium. What does that mean? As thoroughly discussed in my first two books, *Learn Game Theory* and *Practice Game Theory*, a pure-strategy Nash equilibrium occurs only when each player's strategy is the best response to the other's, leaving no incentive for either to change.

The absence of such an equilibrium is what makes mixed strategies important. Without a stable strategy, players find themselves in a tough spot. If one player commits to a single choice like, always picking heads—the other player can quickly exploit that predictability by choosing tails. Practically speaking, players need to think strategically about balancing their options, like choosing courses, which we'll explore in our next example.

Kelsey and Jacob, who played Matching Pennies earlier, suddenly find themselves in an interesting situation: they have to choose courses for their upcoming semester at Harvard University.

Kelsey is interested in "Cultural Psychology" while Jacob is passionate about "Sports Psychology". However, they both prefer to be classmates so they can spend time together because of different intentions. Kelsey wants Jacob to be her study buddy, thinking it's a surefire way to pass her favorite course. Jacob, on the other hand, wants to impress Kelsey, his secret crush, with his intelligence on his desired subject.

		Kelsey	
		Cultural Psychology	Sports Psychology
Jacob	Cultural Psychology	(1, 2)	(0, 0)
	Sports Psychology	(0, 0)	(2, 1)

Based on the table above, it's clear that we have four possible outcomes:

1. **Both Choose Cultural Psychology**

    When Kelsey and Jacob both select Cultural Psychology, it's a win-win. Kelsey enjoys the course and has a study buddy, earning her a 2. Jacob, on the other hand, gets a 1 for being able to spend time with her.

2. **Kelsey Chooses Cultural Psychology, Jacob Chooses Sports Psychology**

    In this scenario, Kelsey chooses Cultural Psychology, hoping to work with Jacob, but he goes for Sports Psychology instead. Kelsey scores a 0, feeling disappointed and missing him, while Jacob also gets a 0, bummed about their separation.

3. **Kelsey Chooses Sports Psychology, Jacob Chooses Cultural Psychology**

    If Kelsey and Jacob chose the courses they didn't like, it's a lose-lose. Neither is happy and scores a 0.

4. **Both Choose Sports Psychology**

    When they both go for Sports Psychology, Kelsey earns a 1 for being with Jacob, even though she's not into the subject. Jacob scores a 2 as he enjoys the course and gets to be with her. While they get to be together, Kelsey feels conflicted about sacrificing her academic goals.

In this example, we have two Nash equilibria: when both choose Cultural Psychology and when both choose Sports Psychology. These scenarios represent the points where neither player can benefit by changing their choice, given the choice of the other.

As mentioned before, Kelsey and Jacob both want to be classmates in the same course. This shows that they really want to work together. However, their differing tastes complicate coordination in this situation.

So, how can Kelsey and Jacob solve their dilemma? They must find the mixed-strategy equilibrium by using the *mixed-strategy algorithm*[91] first. This means solving the probability that Kelsey and Jacob will assign to each course. Let me spare you from the complicated math and proceed with the results:

---

[91] Rutherford, A. (2022). Practice Game Theory : Get a Competitive Edge in Strategic Decision-making Avoid Getting Outplayed, and Maximize Your Gains.

		Kelsey	
		Cultural Psychology (⅔)	Sports Psychology (⅓)
Jacob	Cultural Psychology (⅓)	(1, 2)	(0, 0)
	Sports Psychology (⅔)	(0, 0)	(2, 1)

Based on the table above, Kelsey has the possibility of choosing "Cultural Psychology" two-thirds of the time and "Sports Psychology" one-third of the time. If she does that, Jacob doesn't care which course they take. On the other hand, when Jacob chooses "Cultural Psychology" one-third of the time and "Sports Psychology" two-thirds of the time, Kelsey will feel the same way.

Why? It's simple: both Kelsey and Jacob value spending time together more than their individual preferences for the classes. Kelsey enjoys Cultural Psychology but is willing to compromise to be with Jacob, while Jacob prefers Sports Psychology but also chooses to go with Cultural Psychology to maintain their time together.

Now, let's move forward to *calculating their expected pay-offs* (which I elaborated on in Chapter 4 of *Practice Game Theory*). Based on the result, it looks like that Kelsey and Jacob will end up with an expected payoff of ⅔ each.

		Kelsey	
		Cultural Psychology (⅔)	Sports Psychology (⅓)
Jacob	Cultural Psychology (⅓)	(⅓, ⅔)	(0, 0)
	Sports Psychology (⅔)	(0, 0)	(⅔, ⅓)

This is where it gets interesting: a payoff of ⅔ or ⅓ is a bit of a downer. Why? Because neither Kelsey nor Jacob will feel fulfilled with this outcome—it's less than 1, which is the bare minimum for a decent payoff. This score reflects a compromise that ultimately leads to disappointment. In their case, going for mixed strategies is like saying, "Let's roll the dice and see what happens." It may seem fair on the surface, but it sacrifices their chance to go after what they truly desire, leaving them both feeling unsatisfied.

So, what's the conclusion? Initially, using a mixed strategy might seem like a solid plan because it allows Kelsey and Jacob to balance their preferences. However, upon closer reflection, choosing one class together—like "Cultural Psychology"—would actually benefit them both more.

While mixed strategies may offer a mathematical solution, Kelsey and Jacob's dilemma ended up realizing that sometimes it's smarter to settle on a simple agreement. This guarantees that they both leave satisfied, leading to a better overall outcome.

This game is also known as the Battle of the Sexes.

How To Use Mixed Strategies To Get A Higher Pay

Now, let's talk about a different situation, something more useful in real life: salary negotiations.

Mixed strategies can be incredibly useful in this context. Just like Kelsey and Jacob could benefit from a clear agreement, you can leverage various approaches in salary discussions. By showcasing your unique skills and conducting thorough market research, you can navigate the negotiation process more effectively. This strategic flexibility allows you to adapt your tactics based on the conversation, ultimately helping you land a salary that truly reflects your value.

Let's say there's a fresh graduate named John who is excited to apply for his first job as a software engineer. In his search, he discovers that the average salary for software engineers in 2024 is $123,594, which breaks down to about $59.42 per hour.

To maximize his negotiating power, he decides to use a mixed strategy. He knows that the key rule is to avoid consistently asking for the same salary figure or reiterating the same achievements during negotiations. These predictable responses can make it easy for the employer to anticipate his moves and undervalue his worth.

Fast forward to the initial interview; John speaks about his unique contributions during his internship, such as leading a team that developed a successful ride-hailing app that boosted user engagement by 30%. He backs up his claims with metrics that showcase his impact on productivity and teamwork.

In the final interview, instead of relying on personal achievements alone, John conducts thorough research on industry salary benchmarks. His findings reveal that the most experienced software engineers typically earn around $80 per hour. This research influences him to negotiate for a salary slightly higher than the average. With this data, he presents a compelling case to the hiring manager, showing how his qualifications align with the high-demand skills in the market.

By varying his approach (combining personal accomplishments with detailed industry research), John introduces an element of unpredictability into the negotiation process, leading him to secure a $63 per hour salary, which is definitely better than the average salary of $59.42 per hour.

Applying Mixed Strategies to Other Areas of Life

Now that we've seen how mixed strategies work in salary negotiations, let's consider how to apply these principles in other aspects of life:

- **Sports**

When playing a team sport, instead of always following the same play or strategy, mix it up. Use a combination of offensive and defensive tactics, adapting to the opponent's strengths and weaknesses to keep them guessing. For example, if your basketball opponent excels at defending the perimeter, switch to aggressive drives to the basket to create scoring opportunities.

- **Marketing**

In crafting a marketing campaign, avoid a one-size-fits-all approach. Experiment with various messages, channels, and target audiences. Track the effectiveness of each approach and adjust your strategy based on real-time feedback. For instance, if social media ads resonate more with young professionals than traditional email marketing, allocate more resources to that channel.

- **Personal Relationships**

In conversations or negotiations with friends or family, don't rely solely on your usual arguments or emotional appeals. Vary your approach by incorporating humor, data, or personal stories that resonate with the other person's perspective. For instance, when discussing weekend plans, share a funny memory from a past trip to lighten the mood while also highlighting the benefits of a specific destination.

Ultimately, public goods games underscore the significance of collaboration, pitching in, and making sure everyone benefits collectively. As we move into the next chapter, we'll explore how evolutionary game theory can further enhance your ability to navigate complex social dynamics, including finding a good partner.

Chapter 8: What Evolutionary Game Theory Tells Us About Modern Dating

Francesca, like many others, turned to dating apps in search of a meaningful connection. With each swipe, she encountered new faces and went on numerous dates, yet the outcomes often felt dishearteningly familiar. Too often, she found herself ghosted after the first meeting, left pondering what had gone wrong. It seemed as if some men vanished without explanation, leaving her in a state of confusion and disappointment. On other occasions, she discovered that the man she had just met was juggling conversations with multiple other women. This experience felt all too common, reducing her to just another name on a long list of options.

Then there were the "timer" types—those who engaged in lively conversations but would disappear when it came time to meet in person. They resurfaced days or weeks later, as if keeping her on standby. This left Francesca questioning her worth and whether she was merely an afterthought in their lives. Moreover, there were those who, while presenting themselves as single, were clearly involved with others. Their profiles were carefully constructed facades designed to attract unsuspecting women. Each of these experiences chipped away at her faith in finding someone genuine.

These cycles and experiences led Francesca to wonder why it was so hard to form a real connection in a world filled with digital choices. Fortunately, the principles of Evolutionary Game Theory (EGT) offer a framework to understand this search.

EGT posits that strategies that yield higher rewards tend to spread within a population. This idea has been applied across various fields, including economics and social sciences, showing that competition for limited resources drives selection and adaptation. In the context of dating, EGT recognizes that individuals can adjust their behaviors and strategies over time, favoring those that lead to better outcomes in their relationships.

This perspective reveals that the search for love often follows discernible patterns. With this knowledge, Francesca can approach dating with renewed confidence, positioning herself to find a partner who truly complements her.

History

Game theory began as a way to understand decision-making in competitive situations, focusing on how individuals seek the best outcomes. It was not until later that biologists saw how this idea could help study how living things adapt and evolve together. In 1967, Hamilton pointed out that a creature's success depends on the mix of others in its population, which led to what we now know as Evolutionary Game Theory (EGT).

The early development of Evolutionary Game Theory (EGT) brought significant changes in how key elements of a game—players, strategies, information, and payoffs—were understood. In this context, players, typically animals, were considered pre-programmed to follow specific strategies. They were viewed as carriers of fixed strategies that were genetically determined and unchangeable throughout their lives. Early EGT focused on large animal populations, where an individual's actions had minimal impact on overall strategy success.

Strategies were hard-wired into the animals' genetic makeup, making them phenotypes. Consequently, decision-making information played a limited role, and payoffs were defined in terms of Darwinian fitness, reflecting expected contributions to future generations rather than a hierarchy of preferences.

The main assumption behind evolutionary thinking was that strategies with greater payoffs at a given time would spread more and have a better chance of persisting in the future. Early EGT models proposed that this selection bias toward higher-payoff individuals occurred at the population level through natural selection. This concept aligns with Wallace and Darwin's principles of evolution, summarized as follows:

IF:
- More offspring are produced than can survive and reproduce, and
- Variation within populations affects the fitness (i.e., the expected reproductive contribution to future generations) of individuals, and
- Variation is heritable,

THEN: evolution by natural selection occurs.[92]

The foundational ideas of EGT—that strategies with greater payoffs tend to spread more and that fitness is frequency-dependent—soon transcended biology, influencing other disciplines. In economics, for instance, natural selection was understood as arising from competition for scarce resources or market shares. In social contexts, it

---

[92] Dorin, A. (2009). A review of game theory and its application to evolutionary biology. *Evolution: Education and Outreach*, 2, 548-565. https://doi.org/10.1007/s12052-009-0128-1

was often seen as cultural evolution, reflecting dynamic changes in behavior or ideas over time.

However, Darwinian natural selection was not always ideal for explaining social evolution, especially when individuals could change strategies within their lifetimes. Researchers began focusing on individual strategy choices, where payoffs reflected preferences rather than strict evolutionary fitness. This approach highlighted adaptability and decision-making at the personal level, moving away from direct comparisons of evolutionary success.

The algorithmic view of this process is as follows:

IF:

- Players using different strategies obtain different payoffs, and
- They occasionally revise their strategies (through imitation or reasoning over gathered information), preferentially switching to those providing greater payoffs,

THEN: the frequency of strategies with greater payoffs will tend to increase, potentially altering the future relative success of strategies.[93]

---

[93]Izquierdo, S. S., Izquierdo, L. R., & Sandholm, W. H. (n.d.). Introduction to evolutionary game theory. *Agent-Based Evolutionary Game Dynamics*. Retrieved from

When applied to humans, evolutionary game theory reveals patterns in dating and relationships that are not all that different from the behaviors we see in animals. From selecting a partner to forming alliances within social groups, the strategies we use today—whether intentional or not—are shaped by ancient instincts designed to ensure survival and reproduction.

How EGT Can Enhance Your Love Life

This example illustrates how the theory of Evolutionary Game Theory (EGT) can be applied in practice to enhance one's dating life. John Maynard Smith's introduction of EGT in biological sciences simplifies the intricate world of mating behaviors to help identify a target's "type." Researchers look into the relationship strategies that different species develop—whether that means sticking with one partner, having several, or something in between.

When it comes to romance, EGT sheds light on the strategies folks employ in their pursuit of love. Whether you're dealing with harem-minders,

---

https://math.libretexts.org/Bookshelves/Applied_Mathematics/Agent-Based_Evolutionary_Game_Dynamics_(Izquierdo_Izquierdo_and_Sandholm)/01%3A_Introduction/1.01%3A_Introduction_to_evolutionary_game_theory

monogamists, or sneakers, understanding these behavioral approaches can make the modern dating scene a bit less perplexing. Recognizing these patterns gives you the upper hand, allowing you to make smarter choices in your dating life. In turn, this can pave the way for deeper connections and more fulfilling relationships.

1. **Rock: Harem-Minders**

Harem-minders flourish in settings that embrace casual dating and juggling multiple relationships. They enjoy variety and short-term connections, often turning to platforms like Tinder for new experiences instead of long-term commitments. If you find yourself swiping more for fun than for love, you might be a harem-minder.

Walter Scheidel, a socioeconomic historian, proposes a mating trichotomy for human males by analyzing marriage and sexual practices throughout history. He identifies men who are legally polygamous and sexually active with multiple women—similar to the "harem-minder" lizards in the animal kingdom. These individuals embody the notion that variety is the spice of life, seeking multiple partners without the expectation of commitment.

2. **Scissors: Monogamists**

Monogamists prefer the comfort of exclusive, committed relationships. They value emotional intimacy and the stability that comes with it. These individuals tend to use dating platforms and social settings that focus on finding someone compatible. For those who enjoy a bit of extra hand-holding, apps like Hinge or Coffee Meets Bagel might just fit the bill, offering a chance for meaningful companionship.[94]

3. **Paper: Sneakers**

Sneakers bring a more complicated dynamic to the table. They may appear committed to one partner but often seek casual or extramarital affairs. While platforms like Grindr facilitate short-term flings, those seeking similar experiences with the opposite sex might explore local bars or social events. It's a delicate balancing act of keeping options open while playing the field.

So, who comes out on top in this intricate game of romance? The answer, as it often is, depends on the circumstances. One study argues that institutional monogamy in humans has "group-beneficial effects," primarily because it "reduces the size of the pool of unmarried men," which has been shown to lower criminal activities like rape, murder, robbery, and fraud in societies that culturally embrace harem-minding behaviors.[95]

---

[94] CNET. (2024). Best Online Dating Apps. Article from https://www.cnet.com/tech/services-and-software/best-online-dating-apps/

[95] Dal Borgo, M. (2019, December 17). How game theory can help improve your luck at dating. *BBC Future*. Article from

Importantly, monogamy is not an exclusively male evolutionary strategy. According to zoologist Birgitta Tullberg, groups of female anthropoid primates that began as harem-minders later evolved into monogamous units. Over generations, the signals indicating female ovulation and fertility diminished, prompting males to maintain continuous sexual relationships to ensure paternal certainty. This concealed ovulation evolved in humans as well, further enhancing paternal investment and child-rearing.

As a result, just as scissors beat paper, monogamous individuals often have the advantage over harem-minders, regardless of gender. Yet, much like rock beating scissors, being a "sneaker"—those who engage in casual or extramarital affairs—can sometimes trump monogamous strategies in certain cultures. In societies where high rates of infidelity are reported, the prevalence of sneakers suggests this strategy is effective. Estimates of lifetime infidelity vary widely, from about 14% to 75%, with self-reports likely under-representing the truth.

When it comes to dating apps, the dynamics become even more intriguing. Each platform cultivates its own culture and norms, rewarding different strategies. For instance, many Grindr

---

https://www.bbc.com/future/article/20191217-how-game-theory-can-help-improve-your-luck-at-dating

relationships tend to be short-lived, serving more as a "hookup" app than a venue for long-term connections. Users here often embody the sneaker strategy, which thrives in a predominantly monogamous cultural backdrop.

Conversely, Tinder's user base has a significant portion—about 42%—identifying as sneakers, suggesting that harem-minders may fare better on this platform. Biological anthropologist Helen Fisher advises against following more than nine profiles simultaneously on dating apps, which aligns with the underdog theory: on Tinder, the harem-minder often outperforms the sneaker, similar to paper beating rock.

Ultimately, although harem-minders, monogamists, and sneakers may have equal chances of success in the mating game, each type can encroach upon the others. Monogamists may find themselves with sneakers, raising the risk of infidelity, while harem-minders might get "pinned down" by a more committed partner. Understanding which arenas reward specific types of players can guide you in selecting your game and strategy wisely.

Conclusion

Evolutionary Game Theory (EGT) offers valuable insights into the dynamics of modern dating. It explains how strategies evolve in a population where individuals interact repeatedly, showing that those that yield higher payoffs tend to thrive, while less effective ones fade away.

There are two ways of interpreting the process by which strategies are selected.

- **Biological Systems**: Players are typically pre-programmed to adopt a single strategy throughout their lifetime, with changes in strategy composition occurring through natural selection.

- **Socio-Economic Models**: Players are assumed to adapt their behavior during their lifetime, revising their strategies to favor those that yield greater payoffs at the time of revision.

For individuals like Francesca, understanding these patterns can boost confidence in navigating the dating landscape. By grasping EGT principles, you can make informed choices that enhance your chances of forging deeper connections and more fulfilling relationships.

Chapter 9: A Game Where Everyone Wins (Unless You're a Free Rider)

As someone diagnosed with dyscalculia in the mid-'70s, I always fantasized that my soulmate would be good with numbers. I even wrote it on the back of my notebook. I just felt like I needed a math-capable yin to my number-challenged yang. However, I forgot all about that when I conquered my learning disability and started nailing complex algorithms by fourth grade.

Eventually, I pursued my master's degree and at the time, I was also with my ex-wife, who wanted to be an actress but had a huge ordering problem (which I talked about in my first book). Funnily, our biggest fights always revolved around numbers; she often miscalculated things to the point of believing she had two lovers.

A few months after my divorce, I met my second (and current) wife. I knew she was the one when we had a night out with two friends at Neir's Tavern in New York City. When the bill came, she effortlessly split it in her head without reaching for a calculator. I still remember it very well. Each of us had to pay $16.

In our nerdiest moment together after marriage, we talked about having two children. We always joked that if there were a math-based religion, the number two would be hailed as God. After all, it's the smallest and only even prime number, deserving of its own special worship. We kept that promise and ended up with two lovely kids, who were well into their growing years by the time we faced a fridge dilemma.

There was this one summer when our beloved fridge started to fail. It wasn't a big disaster, but it meant that milk spoiled faster and leftovers didn't last more than a day. We needed to fix the issue quickly, so I gathered everyone in the living room for an emergency family meeting.

In the '90s, the cheapest fridge was around $400, so I gave my family two options: the four of us could each pitch in to buy a new one or try to make do a bit longer and hope the old fridge held up. I thought it would be great for the kids to help out, especially since they had started a lemonade stand in the front yard. I just wanted to teach them the concept of responsibility so they wouldn't be in shock when they reached adulthood.

"If everyone contributes, we can get a new fridge," I said. "Otherwise, we'll have to wait." Maybe you're not a fan of my parenting approach, but aside from my wife and me, the kids used the fridge too. In fact, their little business relied on it.

They needed it to make ice for their lemonades, so I thought it was only fair that they contribute.

My son didn't like the idea, "But I'm saving for a Sony PlayStation!" Meanwhile, my daughter felt conflicted as she had already promised to give all of her earnings to charity. Of course, my wife and I were prepared to contribute more than our share, but I thought if I pushed the kids hard enough, they'd eventually agree.

Because my wife had the final say in all matters, she persuaded me to split the bill between the two of us and buy a new fridge that same day. The kids were happy because their little business won't be affected. My son continued saving for his PlayStation - a commendable effort in and of itself. And my daughter could donate her money to the local cat shelter.

Looking back, I see how easily we fall into the mindset of expecting others to carry the load. I can't blame my kids for wanting to enjoy the perks of a working fridge without chipping in. They were just being kids, after all. If I had been their age, I would have rebelled against chipping in for a fridge. How boring.

It's interesting to think about how this mindset isn't new. If I was born into a wealthy family in Ancient Rome, I'd probably be sipping on free fresh water from the aqueducts[96], thinking it's the most natural thing ever, completely dispassionate towards the backbreaking work slaves undergone to build the thing.

And this pattern extends far beyond ancient times. No matter where you're from, you likely benefit from someone else's hard work without realizing it. Take a moment to think about the roads, hospitals, and parks. They were all built and maintained by laborers for you to use. Sounds great, right? However, this creates a social dilemma if we all want to free-ride on other's efforts while contributing as little as possible ourselves. If that happens, we all risk losing those shared benefits.

History

This idea gets to the heart of what we call **public goods games**. While it has no distinct proponent, its development can be traced back to Garrett Hardin's essay entitled *Tragedy of the Commons*[97]. His story about the shared pasture shows how selfish actions can ruin something that everyone shares. It's a classic example of the "free-

---

[96]Lesso, R. (2024, February 12). How did Romans build aqueducts? TheCollector. https://www.thecollector.com/how-did-romans-build-aqueducts/

[97]Hardin, G. (1968). The tragedy of the Commons. *Science*, *162*(3859), 1243–1248. https://doi.org/10.1126/science.162.3859.1243

rider problem," where people try to get the benefits without doing their part.

The concept evolved into a public goods game, which became closely tied to game theory, particularly the prisoner's dilemma. According to Choi and Bowes, the public goods game and the prisoner's dilemma are equivalent because they both illustrate how cooperation and defection affect payoffs in a group[98], which we'll explore later on in this chapter.

According to Zhang and Tao (2016), the only Nash equilibrium in a public goods game suggests that everyone will choose to free ride, benefiting from the contributions of others without contributing anything themselves[99].

However, when researchers conduct PGG experiments, they observe a different pattern: most participants tend to contribute about half of their resources to the public pool initially. This early generosity is promising, but as the game progresses, people's willingness to contribute often starts to decline. It's as if their initial excitement for cooperation begins to drop, leading them to think,

---

[98]Choi, J., & Bowles, S. (2007). The coevolution of parochial altruism and war. Science, 318(5850), 636–640. https://doi.org/10.1126/science.1144237

[99]Dong, Y., Zhang, B. & Tao, Y. The dynamics of human behavior in the public goods game with institutional incentives. *Sci Rep* 6, 28809 (2016). https://doi.org/10.1038/srep28809

"Why should I keep giving if others aren't?" This change shows a common human experience where motivation can shift over time, highlighting the struggle between individual interests and the well-being of the group.

How It Works

Let's discuss a public goods game with a hypothetical problem. Imagine there are four residents in an apartment building who are deciding whether to contribute to setting up a community Wi-Fi system.

Each resident can chip in $15 to improve the building's Wi-Fi to make the internet faster and more reliable for everyone, giving each person a $10 worth of boost in internet quality. But what's the catch? One person's decision to pay impacts everyone else's benefits, making it a group decision with individual consequences.

Now, let's look at George, one of the residents who's currently taking up a business course. He has to weigh the benefit of a better internet against the cost of contributing. How fast the Wi-Fi gets depends on how many neighbors pitch in, but if George decides to help, he'll have to subtract that $15 from his overall payoff.

Let's say two of George's neighbors, who were practicing legislators, decide to chip in. If

George chooses not to contribute, he'll still enjoy the $10 boost in internet quality from each of the neighbors' contributions, giving them a total benefit of $20—without paying a dime.

Two other players chip in	Alex doesn't chip in (free-rides)	Alex chips in
Benefit from others' contributions	20	20
+ benefit if he contributes	+0	+10
- cost of his contribution	-0	-15
Total	**$20**	**$15**

So based on the table above, if Alex *does* decide to chip in, he'll get an extra $10 benefit from his own contribution (and so will the others), but it'll cost George $15. That means his total benefit is $30, but after subtracting the cost, George is left with a net payoff of $15. Obviously, if George contributes, it helps everyone but he ends up with slightly less compared to free-riding.

When one resident covers the cost to improve the internet, everyone in the building benefits. But this is where the problem comes in: no matter what the other neighbors decide, George always makes out better if he doesn't contribute, even if his neighbors do. In public good games like this, each player can free-ride on the contributions of others, enjoying the benefit without spending anything.

It's like the classic prisoners' dilemma, but with more than two players. Just like in the Wi-Fi problem, one resident's decision affects everyone else. If all the residents focus only on their own payoff, the game hits a Nash equilibrium where no one contributes and the Wi-Fi remains slow for everyone, with payoffs essentially being zero.

Of course, if all the neighbors pitched in, they'd each enjoy significantly faster internet and a payoff of $20. While cooperation would lead to better outcomes for everyone, it's challenging to maintain because there's always the temptation to free-ride, which each person would naturally prefer. (Why pay when you can get it for free, right?)

But let's consider that George decides not to contribute. How can the two residents who *did* chip in prevent him from free-riding? Well, as future policymakers, the two neighbors can propose an effective solution: introducing a membership fee to emphasize the importance of cooperation. By putting this fee in place, George would have to contribute his share, ensuring everyone chips in fairly.

A 2015 study[100] reflects this situation perfectly. Researchers ran public goods games with two groups: university undergraduates and American state legislators. Both groups played by the same rules and had the same incentives.

Each game started with a "table fund," calculated by multiplying the number of players by 100. So, if there were five players, the fund would total 500. Each player then chose an amount between 0 and 100 to take from this fund, which they kept for themselves. After everyone made their choices, the total amount withdrawn was deducted from the table fund, and the leftover was doubled. This doubled total was then divided equally among all players, meaning everyone got their chosen amount plus a share of the remaining fund.

In the end, legislators were found to be more generous and consistent in their contributions than university students. Both groups reacted similarly to changes in time frames, but deliberation had different effects on their gameplay. For students, talking about the game reduced their withdrawals from the common resource significantly—from 24 points without discussion to just 9 points when they could discuss.

---

[100]Butler, D., & Kousser, T. (2015). How Do Public Goods Providers Play Public Goods Games? Legislative Studies Quarterly, 40(2), 211-240. http://dx.doi.org/10.1111/lsq.12073 Retrieved from https://escholarship.org/uc/item/2fr1q8mz

So, here's what I realized from that study: first, communication really helped students cooperate better. Who knew that a little chit-chat could do wonders? And second, this is exactly why the government imposes taxes on us. They've figured out that when we all talk about contributing, we're more likely to pitch in for the greater good.

Using Public Goods Games to Organize Parties

Even if that greater good involves party people, public goods game can come handy.

Let's take Poppy, who decided to organize a Christmas potluck party for her book club, which consisted of 20 people. She's all in, ready to spread the festive spirit, but we all know how it goes: some people love to feast but would rather not lift a finger. Let's say only 10 wanted to contribute, while the other 10 would still be able to eat without bringing anything. Now, that's a classic free-rider problem.

To solve this dilemma, she channels her inner strategist and applies some public goods game principles. First, she sets up a group chat, where she lays down the festive law: the more everyone contributes, the more amazing the feast will be. After all, nobody wants to show up to a party with a sad cheese platter.

She also assigns each person a specific dish category: appetizers, main courses, desserts, and drinks. This way, she makes sure that everyone has a role to play, and no one can sit back and enjoy the spread without putting in their fair share.

Poppy puts in a little motivation by introducing a friendly competition, as well. The person who brings the most popular dish, as voted by the group, will win a fun holiday prize. The effect? Everyone was eager to show off their cooking skills.

On the day of the party, the table is full of delicious dishes, and everyone digs. Poppy's knack for bringing her book club together not only gives them a fantastic meal, but also fosters a warm sense of community that makes the holiday season special. That's the magic of utilizing public goods game knowledge.

Applying Public Goods Games to Other Areas of Life

Though I can't predict the odds of you becoming a party organizer (we all have our unique paths in life), I can say with confidence that at some point, you'll find yourself stepping into the role of a leader. Whether it's at school, work, in your community, or even within your own family. Who knows? You might even end up as president!

But here's the somewhat harsh truth: leading a group can often feel like trying to herd cats, especially when everyone wants to be a free-rider. How can you use the knowledge you just learned in different areas of your life? Here are some practical ways:

- **Workplace Collaboration**

If you find yourself managing a team, set up regular brainstorming meetings where everyone can share their ideas and suggestions. When someone comes up with a particularly good idea, praise them during the session. This kind of recognition not only boosts morale but also inspires others to step up and contribute.

- **Community Engagement**

Consider a neighborhood clean-up day or a block party. When planning, send out a flyer or create a social media post inviting everyone to bring their skills or resources to the table. For instance, one neighbor could provide trash bags, while another might bring snacks and drinks. If everyone pitches in, you'll create a richer experience, like a cleaner park and a fun community barbecue to celebrate the hard work afterward.

- **Family Responsibilities**

Now, this is a bit different from my fridge dilemma earlier because contributions don't always have to involve money. Instead of one person handling all the chores, step up and hold a family meeting to discuss responsibilities. For example, when there's a big event like a holiday, talk about who will take care of decorations, shopping, cooking, and cleaning. Assign specific tasks to each family member and emphasize that teamwork is essential for making the holidays memorable.

All in all, the public goods game shows us an important truth: when people cooperate, everyone benefits. But we can't ignore the free riders who take advantage without contributing. We need to encourage teamwork and responsibility. After all, any group thrives when everyone plays their part. That's how we all win in the end.

If you're still here, congratulations! We've arrived at the final (and most important) chapter of this book, where we'll dive into how game theory can serve as a valuable tool for making informed financial choices.

Chapter 10: Navigating Wealth with Game Theory

In 2000, the UK auction for 3G mobile phone licenses served as a prime example of how game theory could shape high-stakes scenarios, much like a poker game where the stakes were sky high and everyone's got their eye on the pot. Game theory experts Paul Klemperer and Ken Binmore designed the auction with goals of efficient spectrum allocation, promoting competition, and maximizing economic value.

Now, let me tell you, this was no ordinary auction. It was like watching a fast-paced horse race. The bidding unfolded in multiple rounds, with participants engaging in a strategic dance. To stay in the game, bidders either had to hold the highest bid or keep incrementally raising their offers, all while trying to assess the value of each license against the backdrop of competing bids. I remember my old buddy, Tom, who was knee-deep in telecommunications at the time. He'd often joke that these auctions felt more like a circus than a business deal, with everyone juggling numbers and trying to predict the next big act.

As the bidding intensified, the confidence among bidders grew, reflecting a collective understanding of the licenses' value. Initially projected to generate between £2 billion and £3 billion, the auction far exceeded expectations. By early April, total bids reached £10 billion, prompting the first bidder to withdraw, signaling a shift in confidence that influenced subsequent decisions.

After nearly a month of intense back-and-forth, the auction concluded on April 27th, with a jaw-dropping £22.5 billion raised. This outcome not only illustrated the effectiveness of game theory in auction design but also set records that would echo through the industry for years to come.[101]

However, not every story from that auction ended on a high note. The excessive enthusiasm that propelled this bidding frenzy also bore significant consequences. Many telecom companies over-committed financially, driven by that age-old fear of missing out on a lucrative opportunity. I can't help but think of Bob, who once told me about a real estate deal he regretted for years because he didn't stick to his budget. The intense competition led some firms to make bids

---

[101] Jeffery, T. (2021, February 23). What is game theory? Students Economic Portal. Retrieved from
https://medium.com/students-economic-portal/game-theory-e0a2d4af5295

that far exceeded their actual financial capabilities, leaving them in a heap of debt.

As the dust settled, the repercussions were dire. Several companies faced severe financial strain, and the long-term viability of the 3G network came into question. The market ended up flooded with licenses that were too expensive for many players to utilize effectively, creating an environment rife with instability. I remember the conversations at family gatherings, where folks scratched their heads over why 3G wasn't rolling out as quickly as expected, and the answer lay in the numbers that simply didn't add up.

This duality of the auction highlights critical strategies for survival in high-stakes financial environments:

1. **Understanding Limits**: Bidders must recognize their financial limits and avoid getting caught in the competitive frenzy that can lead to poor decision-making. I've always told my kids, "know when to walk away," and that's true in auctions as much as in life.

2. **Collaborative Strategy**: While competition can drive innovation and efficiency, there's often value in strategic alliances. It reminds me of a time when my neighbors and I banded together to negotiate better prices for bulk purchases.

Sometimes, sharing insights can create a more stable market environment.

3. **Adapting to Signals**: It's crucial for investors to adapt their strategies based on market signals. Being able to read the room—recognizing when the bidding environment is becoming unsustainable—can help avoid pitfalls associated with collective overconfidence. Just like in poker, knowing when to fold can save you from losing your shirt.[102]

History

Investing in financial markets can feel overwhelming as every choice holds weighty consequences. Game theory can provide a powerful analytical framework that equips investors with the insights needed to navigate uncertainty effectively. By employing game theory principles, investors can make more informed decisions, optimizing their strategies while anticipating the behaviors of others.

When we discuss financial matters, we can't overlook the ideas of Nash equilibrium and the prisoner's dilemma. While these concepts have

---

[102] Comms Business. (2013, February 20). UK learns lessons from 3G auction. Retrieved from https://www.commsbusiness.co.uk/content/news/uk-learns-lessons-from-3g-auction/

been addressed earlier in the book, it's worth highlighting how they apply to investing, providing valuable insights into how investors can position themselves wisely in this competitive landscape.

The **Nash equilibrium** provides a lens through which investors can identify stable strategies. In financial markets, this means recognizing that each investor's decision impacts the broader market dynamics. For instance, when two investors assess whether to invest in stocks or bonds, the Nash equilibrium occurs when neither investor has an incentive to change their strategy, given the expected behavior of the other. This understanding allows investors to balance their risk and return profiles effectively, ultimately optimizing their asset allocation strategies.

Meanwhile, the **prisoner's dilemma** reminds us of the complications that arise with potential collaboration. Sometimes working together leads to mutual benefits, like when investors cooperate to influence stock prices. However, the temptation to act independently for personal gain creates a risk, emphasizing the importance of trust and communication.

By integrating game theory into financial decisions, from stock market investments to real estate purchases, investors can anticipate competitor actions and adjust their strategies to maximize outcomes. Just like in negotiations—whether it's buying a car or bidding on real estate—

game theory informs tactics that lead to better deals.[103]

Predicting Competitor Moves with Game Theory Models

1. Prisoner's Dilemma.

This model illustrates the conflict between cooperation and self-interest. In business, this model is particularly relevant when companies must choose between competing aggressively and collaborating with one another.

For example, two firms in a competitive market might benefit from maintaining high prices. However, the incentive to undercut each other can lead to reduced profits for both, as they engage in a price war. The prisoner's dilemma emphasizes that, while cooperation could lead to better outcomes for all parties, the fear of being undercut often drives firms to act in their own interest, which can ultimately harm everyone involved.

2. Cournot Model.

---

[103] Benkler, Y., & Nissenbaum, H. (2005). Commons-based peer production and virtue. The Journal of Political Philosophy, 12(2), 208-228. http://dx.doi.org/10.1111/j.1467-9760.2006.00235.x
Retrieved from
https://www.sciencedirect.com/science/article/pii/S1573449805800086

This model focuses on how companies decide their production levels based on competitors' output, leading to an equilibrium where neither firm can improve profits by changing its production strategy. It's especially well-applicable in industries with homogeneous products, like steel or oil. The Cournot Model highlights the interdependence of firms in an oligopoly and underscores the importance of strategic decision-making.

3. Stackelberg Model

Unlike Cournot, the Stackelberg model introduces a sequential decision-making process, where one firm (the leader) sets its output first, and other firms (the followers) respond. This model is prevalent in markets dominated by a major player, such as a leading tech company. The Stackelberg leader can leverage its position by anticipating competitors' reactions to its decisions, which can lead to a competitive advantage. This model illustrates how strategic leadership can shape market dynamics and influence competitors' strategies.[104]

---

[104] FasterCapital. (n.d.). Applying game theory models to predict competitors' moves. Retrieved from https://fastercapital.com/topics/applying-game-theory-models-to-predict-competitors-moves.html

Applying Game Theory to Investment Strategies

Game theory can serve as a helpful guide for investors through the unpredictable and competitive world of finance. Here are a few key tips for applying game theory to investment strategies:

1. **Assess Competition**: It's essential to understand the competitive environment. Analyze potential moves of your competitors, as market participants often react to each other's actions.
2. **Identify Best Responses**: In any strategic interaction, investors must recognize the best responses to their competitors' actions. By doing so, they can adjust their strategies to maximize outcomes.
3. **Utilize Nash equilibrium**: In the market, aiming for a Nash equilibrium ensures that your strategy is stable, given the strategies of others. This keeps you from making rash decisions that could throw off your portfolio.
4. **Collaborate Where Possible**: Markets aren't just about winning—it's also about working together when it makes sense. Forming partnerships or alliances with other investors can benefit everyone in the right situation.

5. **Consider Mixed Strategies**: In volatile markets, mixed strategies prevent predictability, keeping competitors uncertain of your next move and giving you a strategic advantage.
6. **Use Historical Data**: Don't discount the past. By analyzing historical trends, you can inform future decisions, helping you avoid mistakes others have made and making your choices more data-driven.
7. **Prioritize Long-Term Relationships**: Markets reward those who think long term. Building trust with other market participants can lead to more reliable, stable returns over time.
8. **Factor in Behavioral Economics**: Not every market participant is rational. Emotions play a big role in financial decisions. By understanding these behavioral patterns, investors can better predict irrational moves by other market participants.[105]

Conclusion

The 2000 UK 3G mobile phone auction was a clear demonstration of how game theory could influence major financial decisions. By focusing on strategy and understanding market dynamics,

---

[105] FasterCapital. (n.d.). Tips for applying game theory in business. Retrieved from https://fastercapital.com/keyword/tips-applying-game-theory.html

bidders who stuck to their limits made it through, while others who overreached found themselves paying the price. It shows that financial success, whether in auctions, stock markets, or real estate, often depends on balancing ambition with a careful assessment of risks.

Game theory teaches us the value of reading the room—knowing when to push forward and when to pull back. Just like in poker, the key is to stay sharp, anticipate your competitors, and not let emotions steer you into risky decisions. In the end, those who manage to combine clear thinking with strategic moves will navigate financial markets with more success.

Takeaways

Game theory isn't merely an abstract concept confined to academic circles; it's woven into our daily lives, influencing the choices we make from the moment we awaken.

Every morning, we encounter a scenario reminiscent of the **Prisoner's Dilemma**. Imagine you set your alarm for 6:30 a.m. and, in a moment of weakness, you hit that snooze button, thinking, "just five more minutes!" But this isn't just about grabbing a few extra winks; it sets off a domino effect that can send your entire day spiraling. Should you embrace the day ahead and get moving, or indulge in a few more cozy minutes and risk the chaos that follows?

Once you gather your wits and head to the grocery store for that first cup of Joe, **Nash equilibrium** comes into play, as everyone navigates the aisles with a shared understanding and a sense of common benefit. During tough times, **Zero-Sum Games** showcase the stark reality of scarcity; gains for one often mean losses for another. Remember the grocery store madness during the pandemic? If you managed to grab the last pack of toilet paper, someone else had to go without. Such situations remind us that some scenarios boil down to clear winners and losers.

As life gradually returns to normalcy, the **Ultimatum Game** rears its head when it's time to split a check or agree on holiday plans, especially after being glued to the couch for so long. Fairness takes the front seat, showing us that people value justice just as much as reason. Whether it's family or coworkers, a little respect goes a long way in keeping everyone in sync.

And let's not forget social media—if you've ever scrolled through your feed, you know exactly what I mean. The **Keynesian Beauty Contest** is alive and kicking. Many post what they think will impress others. It's amusing how we inhabit a world where appearances often overshadow authenticity.

Mixed Strategies are the backup plans we all keep handy. Think of having a frozen meal or takeout stashed in the fridge for those evenings when home-cooked food feels like a Herculean task. Keep your options open. Flexibility is key, whether you're deciding what to have for dinner or plotting your future.

As we mature and seek meaningful relationships (for those of us who do—relationships can be a real rollercoaster, though some of us are perfectly content with the companionship of a loyal dog), we tap into **Evolutionary Game Theory**.

Long before dating apps, the choices we made in relationships were strategic—a mix of timing, interest, and instinct.

The **Public Goods Game** pops up whenever we decide to lend a hand. Whether it's recycling, helping a neighbor, or pitching in at work, cooperation still holds value. We're all in this together, after all.

Finally, **Game Theory in Money** brings it all home. Every financial decision from budgeting to retirement planning, even investing for a secure future—is a strategic game where foresight and discipline dictate who thrives and who merely scrapes by. This is not just about crunching numbers on a spreadsheet; it's about making informed choices that lay the groundwork for long-term success.

From morning routines to big life decisions, these theories run through our lives like an undercurrent. They're lessons in working with what we've got, making thoughtful choices, and finding value in connection and cooperation – right up to life's final stages. Game theory, in a way, prepares us for life's ultimate transition, reminding us to make each choice count, cooperate where we can, and leave behind something worthwhile.

So here's a heartfelt thank you to all of you—the readers. Whether you're knee deep in a profession, retired, freelancing, raising kids, or taking life as it comes, you took the time to join me on this exploration of game theory. It truly means a lot.

And, of course, a special nod to the game theorists themselves. They've been that quiet force behind creating the frameworks that help us make sense of the decisions, small and significant—that keep the wheels turning.

Now, envision me, your trusty guide, with your favorite glass of wine or beer in hand—here's to life's games and figuring them out as we go along. May the odds, or better yet, the strategies, always be in our favor. Cheers!

Respectfully,
A. R.

Before You Go…

I would be so very grateful if you would take a few seconds and rate or review this book on Amazon. Reviews – testimonials of your experience - are critical to an author's livelihood. While reviews are surprisingly hard to come by, they provide the life blood for me being able to stay in business and dedicate myself to the thing I love the most, writing.

If this book helped, touched, or spoke to you in any way, please leave me a review and give me your honest feedback.

Thank you so much for reading this book.

About the Author

Albert Rutherford

Blind spots can affect our lives without us realizing it. We often try to address our problems, but we rely on incorrect assumptions, faulty analysis, and misguided deductions. This leads to confusion, stress, and annoyance in our personal and professional connections.

Instead of jumping to conclusions prematurely, we can learn to evaluate information correctly and consistently to make better decisions. Developing systems and critical thinking skills can help us collect and assess data, as well as create impactful solutions in any situation.

Albert Rutherford has dedicated his life to finding evidence-based practices for optimal decision-making. His mantra is to ask better questions, to find more accurate answers, and to draw profound insights. In his free time, Rutherford pursues his long-cherished dream of becoming an author. He enjoys spending time with his family, reading the latest science reports, fishing, and pretending to know about wine. He firmly believes in Benjamin Franklin's words, "An investment in knowledge always pays the best interest."

Read more books from Albert Rutherford:

Advanced Thinking Skills

The Systems Thinker Series

Game Theory Series

Critical Thinking Skills

Reference List

Ahlstrom, L. (2023, August 30). Ultimatum game. *INOMICS*. Retrieved from https://inomics.com/terms/ultimatum-game-1538668

arXiv, E.T. from the (2024) How to win at Rock-paper-scissors, MIT Technology Review. Available at: https://www.technologyreview.com/2014/04/30/13423/how-to-win-at-rock-paper-scissors/

Barash, D. (2020, December 30). *The Prisoner's Dilemma = America's Gun Dilemma*. Psychology Today. Retrieved December

Becher, J. (2012, July 27). Why Gas Stations Are So Close To Each Other. Forbes. Retrieved from https://www.forbes.com

Bieber, C., JD. (2024, March 1). States with the worst crime rates. Forbes Advisor. https://www.forbes.com/advisor/legal/criminal-defense/crime-rate-by-state/

Binazir, A. (2011, November 17). Dating and Game Theory: How to make Better decisions in your love life. *HuffPost*. https://www.huffpost.com/entry/how-to-date-dating-and-ga_b_561152

Blackwell, D. et al. (1996) Statistics, probability, and game theory: Papers in honor of David Blackwell. Ithaca, NY, Durham, NC: Cornell University Library ; Duke University Press.

Blais, A., & Nadeau, R. (1996). Measuring strategic voting: A two-step procedure. *Electoral Studies*, *15*(1), 39–52. https://doi.org/10.1016/0261-3794(94)00014-x

Bland, A. R., Roiser, J. P., Mehta, M. A., Schei, T., Sahakian, B. J., Robbins, R. W., & Elliott, R. (2017, June 16). "Cooperative Behavior in the Ultimatum Game and Prisoner's Dilemma Depends on Players' Contributions." *Frontiers in Psychology*. https://www.frontiersin.org/journals/psychology/articles/10.3389/fpsyg.2017.01017/full

Brañas-Garza, P. (2006, July 31). Poverty in Dictator Games: Awakening solidarity. *Journal of Economic Behavior & Organization*, 60(3), 306-320. https://www.sciencedirect.com/science/article/abs/pii/S0167268105001344?via%3Dihub

BusinessDay. (2021, November 11). *Playing the Keynesian beauty contest game on the NSE -*

Businessday NG. Businessday NG. https://businessday.ng/analysis/article/playing-the-keynesian-beauty-contest-game-on-the-nse/

Butler, D., & Kousser, T. (2015). How Do Public Goods Providers Play Public Goods Games? Legislative Studies Quarterly, 40(2), 211-240. http://dx.doi.org/10.1111/lsq.12073 Retrieved from https://escholarship.org/uc/item/2fr1q8mz

Carr, D. (2008, February 12). Who Won the Writers Strike? *The New York Times*. Retrieved from https://www.nytimes.com/2008/02/12/arts/television/12strike.html

Cambridge Dictionary. (n.d.). *Zero-sum game*. https://dictionary.cambridge.org/dictionary/english/zero-sum-game .

Chen, J. (2024 June 5). "Nash equilibrium." Investopedia. https://www.investopedia.com/terms/n/nash-equilibrium.asp.

Choi, J., & Bowles, S. (2007). The coevolution of parochial altruism and war. Science, 318(5850), 636–640. https://doi.org/10.1126/science.1144237

CORE Econ. (n.d.). Strategic interactions: The ultimatum game. Retrieved from https://www.core-econ.org/the-economy/microeconomics/04-strategic-interactions-11-ultimatum-game.html

CORE Econ, *Strategic interactions: The ultimatum game*.

Cornell University (2022 November 2). "Crossing an Intersection and Nash equilibrium." Blog post from https://blogs.cornell.edu/info2040/2022/11/02/crossing-an-intersection-and-nash-equilibrium

COVID-19 deaths | WHO COVID-19 dashboard. (n.d.). Datadot. https://data.who.int/dashboards/covid19/deaths?n=o

CNET. (2024). Best Online Dating Apps. Article from https://www.cnet.com/tech/services-and-software/best-online-dating-apps/

Dal Borgo, M. (2019, December 17). How game theory can help improve your luck at dating. *BBC Future*. Article from https://www.bbc.com/future/article/20191217-how-game-theory-can-help-improve-your-luck-at-dating

Dong, Y., Zhang, B. & Tao, Y. The dynamics of human behavior in the public goods game with institutional incentives. *Sci Rep* 6, 28809 (2016). https://doi.org/10.1038/srep28809

Dorin, A. (2009). A review of game theory and its application to evolutionary biology. *Evolution: Education and Outreach*, 2, 548-565. https://doi.org/10.1007/s12052-009-0128-1

Effectiviology. (n.d.). *Zero-sum bias*. Retrieved from https://effectiviology.com/zero-sum-bias/#Dangers_of_the_zero-sum_bias

Faster Capital. (n.d). *The Limitations of Nash equilibrium*. Retrieved from https://fastercapital.com/topics/the-limitations-of-nash-equilibrium.html.

Faster Capital. (2024 June 19). *Zero-sum game: Winning at all costs – Dominant strategies in zero-sum scenarios*. Retrieved from https://www.fastercapital.com/content/Zero-Sum-Game--Winning-at-All-Costs--Dominant-Strategies-in-Zero-Sum-Scenarios.html#Introduction-to-Zero-Sum-Games

Fehr, E., & Krajbich, I. (2014). "Ultimatum Games." In *Neuroeconomics* (Second Edition, pp. 193-218). https://www.sciencedirect.com/topics/neuroscience/ultimatum-game.

Game Theory in Animal Behavior: Networks Course blog for INFO 2040/CS 2850/Econ 2040/SOC 2090. (2022, September 22). https://blogs.cornell.edu/info2040/2022/09/22/game-theory-in-animal-behavior/

Garrett, K., & Moore, E. (2008). Teaching Mixed Strategy Nash equilibrium to undergraduates. *International Review of Economics Education*, 7(2), 79–87. https://doi.org/10.1016/s1477-3880(15)30088-8

Geiger, A. (2024, July 24). Key facts about Americans and guns. Pew Research Center. https://www.pewresearch.org/short-reads/2024/07/24/key-facts-about-americans-and-guns/

Halton, C. (2022, June 28). Iterated Prisoner's Dilemma: Definition, Example, Strategies. Retrieved from https://www.investopedia.com/terms/i/iterated-prisoners-dilemma.asp

Harsanyi, J. (1967–68) *Manage. Sci.* 14, 159–182, 320–334, 486–502.

Hayes, A. (2024, June 27). Game Theory: A Comprehensive Guide. Retrieved from https://www.investopedia.com/terms/g/gametheory.asp

Hayes, A. (2024, June 27). *Game Theory: A Comprehensive guide.* Investopedia. https://www.investopedia.com/terms/g/gametheory.asp#toc-useful-terms-in-game-theory

Hardin, G. (1968). The tragedy of the Commons. *Science, 162*(3859), 1243–1248. https://doi.org/10.1126/science.162.3859.1243

Holt, C. A., & Roth, A. E. (2004 March 15). "The Nash equilibrium and market design." Proceedings of the National Academy of Sciences, 101(47), 16820-16825. Research article from https://www.pnas.org/doi/10.1073/pnas.0308738101.

Holt, C., Johnson, C., & Schmidtz, D. (2015). Prisoner's Dilemma experiments. In *Cambridge University Press eBooks* (pp. 243–264). https://doi.org/10.1017/cbo9781107360174.014

Houser, D., & McCabe, K. (2014, Pages 19-34). "Ultimatum Games." In *Neuroeconomics* (Second Edition pp. 19-34). https://www.sciencedirect.com/topics/neuroscience/ultimatum-game.

International Banker. (2021, September 29). *The Dotcom Bubble Burst (2000)*. https://internationalbanker.com/history-of-financial-crises/the-dotcom-bubble-burst-2000/

iMotions. (n.d.). The ultimatum game: Theory, variations, and implications. Retrieved from https://imotions.com/blog/learning/research-fundamentals/the-ultimatum-game/

"Introduction to Economic Analysis." (n.d.). "Games and Strategic Behavior: Nash equilibrium." LibreTexts. https://socialsci.libretexts.org/Bookshelves/Economics/Introduction_to_Economic_Analysis/16%3A_Games_and_Strategic_Behavior/16.02%3A_Nash_Equilibrium.

Izquierdo, S. S., Izquierdo, L. R., & Sandholm, W. H. (n.d.). Introduction to evolutionary game theory. *Agent-Based Evolutionary Game Dynamics*. Retrieved from https://math.libretexts.org/Bookshelves/Applied_Mathematics/Agent-Based_Evolutionary_Game_Dynamics_(Izquierdo_Izquierdo_and_Sandholm)/01%3A_Introduction/1.01%3A_Introduction_to_evolutionary_game_theory

J. Rogers (2018 April 27) "The Game Theory Glitch in A Beautiful Mind," *Law & Liberty*, Essay from https://lawliberty.org/the-game-theory-glitch-in-a-beautiful-mind/.

Jeffery, T. (2021, February 23). What is game theory? Students Economic Portal. Retrieved from https://medium.com/students-economic-portal/game-theory-e0a2d4af5295

Jentsch, P., Anand, M., & Bauch, C. T. (2020). Prioritising COVID-19 vaccination in changing social and epidemiological landscapes. *medRxiv (Cold Spring Harbor Laboratory)*. https://doi.org/10.1101/2020.09.25.20201889

Kaushik, P. (2020, March 17). Covid-19 and the Prisoner's Dilemma. *Asia Times*. https://asiatimes.com/2020/03/covid-19-and-the-prisoners-dilemma/

Kellermann, A. L., Somes, G., Rivara, F. P., Lee, R. K., & Banton, J. G. (1998). Injuries and deaths due to firearms in the home. *Journal of Trauma and Acute Care Surgery*, *45*(2), 263–267. https://doi.org/10.1097/00005373-199808000-00010

Kingston,M. (2023 September 12) "*Understanding Nash equilibrium in Game Theory*." https://builtin.com/data-science/nash-equilibrium.

Lehmann, J. (2024) *The Battle of Austerlitz and the utility of game theory for operational analysis, E.* Available at: https://www.e-ir.info/2024/04/09/the-battle-of-austerlitz-the-utility-of-game-theory-for-operational-analysis/

Lesso, R. (2024, February 12). How did Romans build aqueducts? TheCollector. https://www.thecollector.com/how-did-romans-build-aqueducts/

Loewen, P. J., Hinton, K., & Sheffer, L. (2015). Beauty contests and strategic voting. *Electoral Studies, 38*, 38–45. https://doi.org/10.1016/j.electstud.2015.01.001

Louie, D. (2019, April 25). Is game theory the secret to winning "Jeopardy!"? ABC7 San Francisco. https://abc7news.com/james-holzhauer-jeopardy-on-game/5269190/

Majaski, C. (2023 August 13). "What's the Difference Between a Dominant Strategy Solution and a Nash equilibrium Solution?" Investopedia. https://www.investopedia.com/ask/answers/071515/what-difference-between-dominant-strategy-solution-and-nash-equilibrium-solution.asp.

Majumdar, M. (2018, March 8). How Nash equilibrium applies in traffic signals. Retrieved from https://www.linkedin.com/pulse/how-nash-equilibrium-applies-traffic-signals-mrittika-majumdar/

Market Business News. (n.d.). *Zero-sum game: Definition and meaning.* Retrieved from https://marketbusinessnews.com/financial-glossary/zero-sum-game-definition-meaning/

Mauersberger, F., & Nagel, R. (2018). Levels of Reasoning in Keynesian beauty Contests: A Generative framework. In *Handbook of computational economics* (pp. 541–634). https://doi.org/10.1016/bs.hescom.2018.05.002

McDonough, J. (2021, May 14). Berlin Experiences. The Potsdam Conference: July 23rd, 1945 - Koenigsberg, Prussia. Retrieved from https://berlinexperiences.com/the-potsdam-conference-july-23rd-1945-koenigsberg-prussia/

McHugh, L. (n.d.). *Chapter 10: Game theory and strategic decision making.* McGraw-Hill Education. Retrieved from https://highered.mheducation.com/sites/dl/free/0077108310/329284/CH10.pdf

Miller, *The writer's strike and game theory.*

"Mukund" (2021 January 17). "A Beautiful Theory: A Beautiful Mind—Understanding Nash equilibrium." Article from https://reachoutmukund.medium.com/a-beautiful-theory-a-beautiful-mind-understanding-nash-equilibrium-f7646e9dfda 1.

Nitkin, K. (2023, October 6). *A game theory strategy to fight political gridlock*. Arts & Sciences Magazine. https://magazine.krieger.jhu.edu/2023/05/a-game-theory-strategy-to-fight-political-gridlock/

Npr. (2011, January 12). Our cute animal experiment, explained. NPR. https://www.npr.org/sections/money/2011/01/11/132838904/the-tuesday-podcast-our-cute-animal-experiment-explained

Nsut, I. G. T. S. (2021, December 9). Keynesian Beauty Contest - The Indian Game Theory Society, NSUT - Medium. Medium. Retrieved from https://medium.com

Pathak, S. (2024 August 21.). *Zero-sum game*. Wall Street Mojo. Blog from https://www.wallstreetmojo.com/zero-sum-game/

Page, L. (2023, May 5). The true story of the birth of the prisoner's dilemma. *Optimally Irrational*. https://www.optimallyirrational.com/p/the-true-story-of-the-birth-of-the

Pilat D., & Sekoul D. (2021). Game Theory. The Decision Lab. Retrieved August 19, 2024, from https://thedecisionlab.com/reference-guide/economics/game-theory

Prisoner's Dilemma: What Game Are you Playing? (2020, February 22). Farnam Street. https://fs.blog/prisoners-dilemma/

Quora Contributor. (2014 July 16). "Nash equilibrium Explained." Quora. https://www.quora.com/Nash-Equilibrium-Explained.

Research Video: The economic engineer comes to the Keynesian Beauty. (2021, August 30). Retrieved from https://bse.eu/news/research-video-economic-engineer-comes-keynesian-beauty-contest

Rutherford, A. (2022). Practice Game Theory : Get a Competitive Edge in Strategic Decision-making Avoid Getting Outplayed, and Maximize Your Gains.

Semenza, D. (2022, June 21). *More Guns, More Death: The Fundamental Fact that Supports a Comprehensive Approach to Reducing Gun Violence in America | Rockefeller Institute of Government*. Rockefeller Institute of Government. Retrieved October 19, 2024, from https://rockinst.org/blog/more-guns-more-death-the-fundamental-fact-that-supports-a-comprehensive-approach-to-reducing-gun-violence-in-america/

Starmer, C. (2014, July 18). "Nudge novelty has worn off, but we still need behavioural economics." *The Conversation.* https://theconversation.com/nudge-novelty-has-worn-off-but-we-still-need-behavioural-economics-29514.

Sullivan, M. (2024, March 29). President Nixon signs legislation banning cigarette ads on TV and radio. *HISTORY* https://www.history.com/this-day-in-history/nixon-signs-legislation-banning-cigarette-ads-on-tv-and-radio

Talwalkar, P. (n.d.). *The joy of game theory*. Book. Retrieved from https://pdfcoffee.com/presh-talwalkar-the-joy-of-game-theory-pdf-free.html

Team, C. (2023, November 22). Nash equilibrium. Retrieved from https://corporatefinanceinstitute.com/resources/economics/nash-equilibrium-game-theory

Team, I. (2024, June 16). What Is the Prisoner's Dilemma and How Does It Work? Retrieved from https://www.investopedia.com/terms/p/prisoners-dilemma.asp

The Keynesian Beauty Contest - the Decision Lab. (n.d.). Retrieved from https://thedecisionlab.com/reference-guide/psychology/the-keynesian-beauty-contest

The many faces of strategic voting: tactical behavior in electoral systems around the world. (2018). The Library of Congress. https://www.loc.gov/item/2018055286

The Writer's Strike and Game Theory. James D. Miller. 04 Jan 2008. Web.

"Ultimatum Game." Wikipedia, The Free Encyclopedia. https://en.wikipedia.org/wiki/Ultimatum_game.

What Are the 5 Types of Game Theory? An In-Depth Look into Applying Them to Your Business. (n.d.). https://gamify.outfieldapp.com/gamification/business/sales/learning/what-are-the-5-types-of-game-theory

Wijaya, C. Y. (n.d.). Are We Undervaluing Simple Models? - KDnuggets. Retrieved from https://www.kdnuggets.com/are-we-undervaluing-simple-models.

www.ingramcontent.com/pod-product-compliance
Lightning Source LLC
Chambersburg PA
CBHW071455220526
45472CB00003B/812